NATIVE NATION PROJECT

OTHER BOOKS BY LARISSA FASTHORSE PUBLISHED BY TCG

The Thanksgiving Play / What Would Crazy Horse Do?

NATIVE NATION PROJECT

LARISSA FASTHORSE
AND MICHAEL JOHN GARCÉS

THEATRE COMMUNICATIONS GROUP   NEW YORK   2025

Native Nation Project is copyright © 2025 by Larissa FastHorse and Michael John Garcés

Urban Rez, Native Nation, and *Wicoun* are copyright © 2025 by Larissa FastHorse and Michael John Garcés

Foreword is copyright © 2025 by Peter Howard
Hunger for Culture: Reflections on the Making of Urban Rez is copyright © 2025 by Clementine Bordeaux, Kenny Ramos, and Arianna Taylor
"Superheroes on Native Land" by Todd London was adapted from a three-part essay series of the same title originally published on AmericanTheatre.org, in November and December of 2023. Adapted and reprinted by permission of Theatre Communications Group.
"How an 'Urban Rez' Grew into a Native Nation" by James E. Garcia was originally published on AmericanTheatre.org on May 21, 2020. Adapted and reprinted by permission of Theatre Communications Group.

Native Nation Project is published by Theatre Communications Group, Inc., 520 Eighth Avenue, 20th Floor, Suite 2000, New York, NY 10018-4156

All rights reserved. Except for brief passages quoted in newspaper, magazine, radio or television reviews, no part of this book may be reproduced in any form or by any means, electronic or mechanical, including photocopying or recording, or by an information storage and retrieval system, without permission in writing from the publisher.

Professionals and amateurs are hereby warned that this material, being fully protected under the Copyright Laws of the United States of America and all other countries of the Berne and Universal Copyright Conventions, is subject to a royalty. All rights, including but not limited to, professional, amateur, recording, motion picture, recitation, lecturing, public reading, radio and television broadcasting, and the rights of translation into foreign languages are expressly reserved. Particular emphasis is placed on the question of readings and all uses of this book by educational institutions, permission for which must be secured from the authors' representatives: Leah Hamos, The Gersh Agency, 41 Madison Avenue, 29th Floor, New York, NY 10010, (212) 997-1818 and Jonathan Mills, Paradigm Talent Agency, 810 Seventh Avenue, Suite 205, New York, NY 10019, (212) 897-6400.

TCG books are exclusively distributed to the book trade by Consortium Book Sales and Distribution.

Library of Congress Control Number: 2025035782 (print and ebook)
ISBN 978-1-63670-247-6 (paperback) / ISBN 978-1-63670-248-3 (ebook)
A catalog record for this book is available from the Library of Congress.

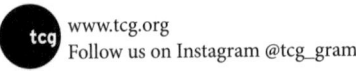
www.tcg.org
Follow us on Instagram @tcg_gram

Book design and composition by Lisa Govan
Cover art and design by Paul Molina

First Edition, November 2025

CONTENTS

Foreword *by Peter Howard*   vii

A Note from the Authors   xiii

HUNGER FOR CULTURE: REFLECTIONS ON
THE MAKING OF URBAN REZ
by Clementine Bordeaux, Kenny Ramos, and Arianna Taylor   1

URBAN REZ   9

HOW AN "URBAN REZ" GREW INTO A NATIVE NATION
by James E. Garcia   85

NATIVE NATION   91

SUPERHEROES ON NATIVE LAND
by Todd London   181

WICOUN   187

FOREWORD

Peter Howard

The gifts traveled in backpacks, in checked baggage, or in the trunks of rental cars: pistachios and dried apricots from California orchards, small pieces of art or jewelry made by California Native artists, maybe some little jars of local honey. Larissa made sure we carried gifts.

The gifts were offered in gratitude to our hosts and partners across Southern California, Arizona, and South Dakota—gratitude for invitation, for hospitality, for trust, for helping us meet and speak with people in their communities. The gifts were small tokens of appreciation from the land and people of Los Angeles, our home base, to the people who helped make this work happen. These plays began as an exchange of gifts.

At every stop on these journeys, generous people shared stories and perspectives with Larissa, Michael, and a varying assortment of colleagues—including, at times, myself. In conversations at cafés and kitchen tables, schools and community centers, tribal offices and pow wows, we heard about family and work, past and future, sources of worry, sources of connection, sources of joy, outrage, laughter, pride.

FOREWORD

These three plays—this unintended trilogy—would not exist without the generosity of everyone who stepped forward, sat in a circle with us and joined a conversation.

In many of these conversations, there were recurring moments. "I'm Larissa FastHorse and I'm a playwright. I'm Sicangu Lakota from Rosebud. I'm here with my friend and director Michael Garcés and we're writing a play." At some point later in the conversation: "We want the play to feel true for you, your people, your communities. We can't do it without you. What should this play be about?" And at some point before the end of the conversation: "Thank you. We'll keep you posted on ways to stay involved. Please know that we will not use your words or your ideas without your permission. And you will always have the right to say no to anything that we include."

I was in the cast of all three of these plays as they made their way through rehearsal and into performance. As a founding ensemble member of Cornerstone, the theater company that produced or co-produced all three, I have been making theater in collaboration with rural and urban communities of many sorts since 1986. These Native Nation plays hold a unique and transformative place in that long history of engaged artmaking. They were co-created by a Native playwright and performed by large, predominantly Native casts—many people acting for the first time. The productions highlighted the work of Indigenous designers, musicians, visual artists. They were not staged in traditional theater spaces. Rather, they unfolded on land and in spaces that were home to the people whose stories were being told.

Cornerstone is part of a rich and growing field. We work alongside many other individual artists and arts organizations committed to challenging entrenched ideas around who gets to be part of creative process and whose stories get told. There are so many reasons why a person might feel distant or even excluded from opportunities to participate in theater-making in our country. Our work can bridge some of that distance by welcoming newcomers into artistic practice. Our work is infinitely enriched by centering bodies and narratives that might otherwise go unseen and unheard. *Native Nation Project* has been an opportunity to reflect on and sometimes shift our practice as artists who create theater with, for, and about communities.

FOREWORD

The invitation is key. For years, Cornerstone used the term "story circle" to describe community conversations in our script development process. Flyers and social media posts would invite potential participants: "Join us. Share your story. Have a snack. No experience required." The story circle is an honored term of practice in our field, in large part thanks to the work of John O'Neal, founder of Junebug Productions. But midway through our Arizona process, we received a gentle reminder from an elder: Story is sacred. And for Native communities who have experienced extraction and theft of story by outsiders for generations, inviting people to a "story circle" was not likely to encourage attendance or build trust. We began to use the term "talking circle" from that point on and continue to use it in both Native and non-Native contexts.

The land is part of the story. Of course, we want to choose performance venues that are welcoming, accessible, safe, and comfortable for all audiences, especially those who don't often attend live theater. In production, the Native Nation plays offered reminders of how venue choice can color or complicate the narrative itself. Each of the three plays was performed in more than one place. Each piece of land spoke with a distinct voice. We opened *Urban Rez* in downtown Los Angeles, where passing Gold Line Metro trains forced us to stop speaking for a few moments until we could be heard again. Then we moved the show several miles west to Kuruvungna Springs, where water still gurgles quietly on land that has been preserved and protected by the Gabrielino-Tongva people, the original inhabitants of the Los Angeles Basin. We first performed *Native Nation* on the tribal land of the Salt River Pima-Maricopa Indian Community, then moved it to the grounds of the former Phoenix Indian School, a boarding school closed by the federal government in 1990 after nearly one hundred years in operation. *Wicoun* was performed in seventeen different locations across South Dakota, on and off reservation land, from tribal gyms to municipal bandshells. For audiences and actors, Native and non-Native, every venue offered a different opportunity to consider our relationship to the land we are standing on while we watch or perform a play.

Collaboration across difference builds community. I can think of no better way to get to know someone than to try to create something with them. American Indian viewpoints are far from monolithic, and each of these plays highlights diversity of perspective within and among Native communities. We were all challenged in production to work with and learn from people with very different experiences from our own. The *Urban Rez* rehearsal process brought together representatives of fifteen different tribal Nations. *Native Nation* wrestled with the reality of twenty-two federally recognized tribal Nations in the state of Arizona, each with its own language, culture, history. *Wicoun* acknowledged the multiplicity within the Oceti Sacowin, and distinctions between Lakota, Dakota, and Nakota identities. Each cast was diverse in other important ways: age, degree of formal education, sexuality, gender identity, spiritual and religious practices, languages spoken, urban or rural background, proximity or distance from homelands. I think it's fair to say that everyone in each process was spending time with someone out of their comfort zone in some way. Collaboration seeds understanding.

And then there was me, "the white guy" in all three productions, as Larissa often (and accurately) describes me. I was grateful to be included in the mix of humanity on stage. I know my characters had dramaturgical function, representing some of the power that white people still hold in the lives of Native communities. I hope that my presence felt like an invitation for white audience members to see themselves in these stories somehow. I have learned an essential truth from these plays: If you're alive on this land we call the United States, you're living on Native ground. We're part of the story, even if our role is one that we'd rather avoid thinking about. In *Urban Rez*, as I moved through the crowd dressed in full Uncle Sam drag, complete with a wispy white goatee and star-spangled top hat, I encountered more than one strategically raised middle finger from Native audience members. Within the playfulness of performance, I understood in a new, visceral way the still-present weight of brutal history.

I have learned other truths from my time with the plays and people of *Native Nation Project*. Humor is resistance. Language is power. Elders and children first. Be the best guest you can be. Humility helps. Always end with a song and a circle dance, and invite the audience to join in.

I'll never know why some folks stepped into the Native Nation process, showed up at a talking circle or an audition or in an audience in L.A., Arizona, or the Northern Plains. I know that their presence and participation were gifts to these plays, which would not exist without them. In dressing rooms and backstage chats, I learned that some of my castmates found reconnection with land, language, and culture in this process, in ways small and large, while others grew in confidence as activists and artists as they practiced speaking with voices that could be heard across a parking lot or in the back row of a tribal gym.

Others found some new sense of community that they didn't have before. I know I did.

Los Angeles, CA
July 2025

PETER HOWARD is a founding member of the Los Angeles–based Cornerstone Theater Company. With Cornerstone, he has collaborated with dozens of urban and rural communities across the US since 1986, working as a performer, playwright, and director to create theater rooted in community identity, creativity, and concerns. Peter also works as a teaching artist, program designer, and facilitator of community dialogue in a variety of youth, university, and community arts settings. Peter was born and raised in Massachusetts.

A NOTE FROM THE AUTHORS

In working on these three projects, Larissa was credited as "playwright" and Michael as "director." While each of us took the lead in our respective roles, the creative partnership on these projects was highly collaborative and porous, with few boundaries in terms of conception and execution of the content, style, and structure of the play and production, from the initial period of engagement with community through opening—and beyond. We consider these plays and the productions we made as the fruit of our shared authorship, always and crucially in necessary collaboration with the communities with and for which they were made.

—*LFH and MJG*

HUNGER FOR CULTURE: REFLECTIONS ON THE MAKING OF *URBAN REZ*

Clementine Bordeaux, Kenny Ramos, and Arianna Taylor

Two performers stand on a stage, take a breath, look at each other, and then turn to the crowd and declare, "HUNGER FOR CULTURE!" They were starring in the 2016 world premiere of *Urban Rez*, an Indigenous-led production written by Larissa FastHorse (Sicangu Lakota). At the time, the play was significant for featuring a predominantly Indigenous cast and addressing cultural yearning in a city that often overlooks Indigenous communities, such as the Tongva, Chumash, Acjachemen, and Tataviam. Produced by Cornerstone Theater Company, and directed by Michael John Garcés, the community-centric storytelling process fostered a committed engagement with Indigenous narratives in American theater, serving as an entry point for understanding the complexities of our identity as urban and reservation-raised performers.

In 2021 we published a more extended version of this article, "Hunger for Culture: Navigating Indigenous Theater," in the *Transmotion* journal.[1] The original essay, authored by we three performers from the show—each of whom identified as queer or Two-Spirit,

---

1. Clementine Bordeaux, Kenny Ramos, and Arianna Taylor, "Hunger for Culture: Navigating Indigenous Theater," *Transmotion* 7, no. 1 (2021): 82–109. https://doi.org/10.22024/UniKent/03/tm.965

and as Lakota, Kumeyaay (Iipai), and Apache—reflected on how *Urban Rez* shifted the discourse around performance and community representation. Indigenous creativity was embedded throughout the creation of *Urban Rez*: From the community engagement process, script production, rehearsal process, and premiere, the show asserted self-representation against settler-colonial frameworks and integrated narratives that remain marginalized in mainstream theater.[2] Almost a decade later, we as co-authors reflect on how the production reshaped discussions on performance and representation, making *Urban Rez* a pivotal moment in our journeys of cultural affirmation and performance.

Part of Cornerstone Theater Company's "Hunger Cycle," *Urban Rez* challenged conventional narratives, highlighting themes of belonging and representation through discussions of sovereignty, tribal identity, and place. *Urban Rez* confronted settler-colonial narratives and uplifted Indigenous voices, positioning itself as an act of visual sovereignty.[3] We portrayed complex characters without conforming to stereotypes, making *Urban Rez* a significant theatrical experience that allowed us to embrace our Indigenous identities without compromising the nuances of tribal life. The production aimed for inter-reflexivity among the co-authors, cast, and community regarding Indigenous identity and the urban experience.

The show resonated with the community's desire for genuine storytelling by creating a space that was familiar to tribal communities but unfamiliar to American theater. *Urban Rez* diverged from typical theater processes by integrating communal narratives. Talking circles were utilized to gather personal experiences from Indigenous individuals in the Los Angeles Basin.[4] This collaborative approach yields a nonlinear storytelling format, enabling performers to engage dynamically with a standing audience. The per-

---

2. When we utilize the term "settler-colonial" we signal to the term popularized by settler scholar Patrick Wolfe (2006) and the further honing of that concept by Indigenous scholars like Audra Simpson (2016), J. Kēhaulani Kauanui (2016), and Shannon Speed (2017).

3. Jolene Rickard et al., "Sovereignty: A Line in the Sand," *Aperture* no. 139 (1995): 50–59.

4. Cornerstone Theater Company utilizes a "story circle" methodology; learn more by visiting their website: https://cornerstonetheater.org/projects/services.

formance space was situated among the audience and often featured multiple storylines and dialogues happening simultaneously. The multivocal nature of the production often left the crew uncertain about the outcome, yet it opened new experiences for the audience, cast, and crew. The production emphasized accountability and reciprocity among the playwright, cast, crew, and audience. Although uncomfortable to attend, the atmosphere lent itself to an engaging performance that centered on what it might be like at a community gathering rather than a typical staged production.

Playwright Larissa FastHorse aimed to challenge stereotypes like the "noble savage" and "Indian princess," which harm Indigenous representation.[5] *Urban Rez* featured diverse characters (in terms of age, gender expression, and locale) representing fourteen tribal nations. Our identities were woven into the performance, enabling us to resist colonial views of tribal identity and challenge images often portrayed as "othered" on stage. Longstanding historical critiques of tribal stereotypes highlight the adverse effects of these representations on Indigenous identities, signaling the need for more inclusive dialogues in both theater and media.[6] *Urban Rez* created a space for radical imagination and decolonization, featuring characters that reflect authentic experiences tied to ancestry and community.

Cornerstone Theater Company, throughout the production, actively supported an Indigenous process through what we would articulate as relational and grounded in tribal autonomy.[7] *Urban Rez* delved into issues of sovereignty through the character Max, a non-federally recognized California Native artist struggling to gain federal recognition, in order to sell his art under the Indian Arts and Crafts Act of 1990. Max's journey highlights the conflict

---

5. Jacqueline Kilpatrick's "Celluloid Indians: Native Americans and Film" (1999) illustrates that stereotypes of tribal people manifest in three ways: first, through the establishment of a mental category utilizing terms like "dumb"; second, through oversexualization of characters either in a romantic or violent staging; and third, through an overt mysticism attributed to spiritual connections.

6. Here we signal to scholars who analyze representation: Deloria (1998); Denetdale (2006); Fryberg et al. (2008); Kilpatrick (1999); Raheja (2011); Rifkin (2011).

7. We reference Indigenous Studies scholars who utilize relationality as a concept to explain kinship practices that demonstrate accountability and reciprocity: Littletree, Belarde-Lewis, and Duarte (2020); Moreton-Robinson (2017); Wilson (2008).

between federal definitions of identity and the vitality of tribal connections, which are often overlooked by mainstream theater. Max's journey in the play centered on his struggle for federal recognition but ultimately revealed the importance of community over external validation. Fundamentally, he learned that relationships within his community are more valuable than recognition from non-Native systems.

Throughout the production, *Urban Rez* was a demonstration of kinship, as defined by Acjachemen and Tongva scholar Charles Sepulveda's ideas of being a guest.[8] Our kinship with the land was highlighted through significant locations for the Tongva, which addressed their history and experiences of violence while providing a moment of Indigenous resistance. The first performance site was located under a bridge downtown, which had been a site of forced labor for the local tribal community. Our performance there brought about contradictions, with the non-Native community and local Indigenous voices viewing the location differently. Performances at sites like Kuruvungna Springs drew new audiences to a hidden gem in West Los Angeles, while causing a stir among local settlers who dismissed the importance of the springs. Overall, the production demonstrated the challenges of community-based theater and the joys of blending moments of shared tears with abundant laughter.

At the end of an *Urban Rez* performance, a Tongva auntie thanked us, saying, "I'm so glad this wasn't Indian *Romeo and Juliet*."[9] Her comment underscored the common deficient portrayals in Indigenous narratives, praising our effort to avoid such tropes. For example, Acjachemen culture bearer Jacque Nuñez expressed on social media how meaningful it was to see their unrecognized California tribe's journey represented accurately and authentically.[10] Nuñez and Virginia Carmelo had earlier presented Larissa with a

---

8. Charles Sepulveda, "Our Sacred Waters: Theorizing Kuuyam as a Decolonial Possibility," *Decolonization: Indigeneity, Education & Society* 7, no. 1: Indigenous Peoples and the Politics of Water (2018): 40–58.

9. We choose not to identify our relative because of privacy and use of their informal statement.

10. Jacque Nuñez, comment on Cecelia Phoenix's photo, Facebook, May 24, 2016, 12:14 A.M. Accessed November 9, 2020.

clapper stick for Tongva song-making at Kuruvungna Springs. As guests (and to be honest, settlers), we strived to center tribal narratives without diminishing the complexity of our lived experiences. As the start of the trilogy of plays at the intersection of community-based work, Cornerstone Theater Company, and tribal communities, *Urban Rez* laid the foundation for Larissa FastHorse and Michael John Garcés to shine as collaborators to this day. As Lakota, Kumeyaay (Iipai), and Apache relatives, we understood the importance of always centering tribal voices without apology.

CLEMENTINE BORDEAUX is an enrolled member of the Sicangu Lakota Oyate (Rosebud Sioux tribe) and was raised on the Pine Ridge Reservation (South Dakota). Clementine is currently an Assistant Professor in the History of Art and Visual Culture at the University of California, Santa Cruz. Clementine's research interests include the use of Indigenous relationality, Indigenous feminisms, Oceti Sakowin (Lakota/Dakota/Nakota) creative practices and visual cultures, as well as community-based participatory research. Clementine is a former board member for Cornerstone Theater Company (Los Angeles, CA) and collaborates regularly with Racing Magpie (Rapid City, SD).

KENNY RAY RAMOS is an Iipai/Kumeyaay theater practitioner from the Barona Band of Mission Indians and was raised on the Barona Indian Reservation in southern California. They are an ensemble member at Cornerstone Theater Company, where they worked on all of the Native Nation Trilogy plays. Kenny is passionate about making theater that centers Native perspectives and asserts tribal sovereignty, and they are interested in the relationship between theater-making and nation-building. Kenny holds a BA in American Indian studies from the University of California—Los Angeles and is currently pursuing an MFA at the Institute of American Indian Arts.

ARIANNA TAYLOR is a proud member of the White Mountain Apache Tribe from Whiteriver, Arizona, now living in Los Angeles, CA. She is currently studying cosmetology and has big dreams of becoming a successful drag performer and starting her own business. Arianna is also writing a book called *Dreams Beyond the Border*, which shares her personal journey and hopes for the future. Passionate about creativity and expression, she is exploring opportunities in acting and modeling. Arianna's mission is to inspire others through authenticity, art, and ambition while representing her community with pride and purpose.

BIBLIOGRAPHY

Arcos, Betto. "*Urban Rez* Explores What It Means to Be Native American." *All Things Considered*. National Public Radio, April 30, 2016, https://www.npr.org/2016/04/30/476306720/-urban-rez-explores-what-it-means-to-be-native-american.

Bordeaux, Clementine; Kenny Ramos; and Arianna Taylor. "Hunger for Culture: Navigating Indigenous Theater." *Transmotion* 7, no. 1 (2021): 82–109, https://doi.org/10.22024/UNIKENT/03/TM.965.

Brandes, Philip. "Review: With L.A. State Historic Park as Its Stage, Cornerstone Unfurls Tales of Native American Identity." *Los Angeles Times*, April 14, 2016, https://www.latimes.com/entertainment/arts/la-et-cm-urban-rez-review-cornerstone-theatre-20160413-story.html.

Clemenco, Sage Alia. "*Urban Rez*: Voices of Native American Actors." *PBS SoCal*, April 22, 2016, https://www.pbssocal.org/shows/artbound/urban-rez-voices-of-native-american-actors.

Cornerstone Theater Company, https://cornerstonetheater.org/.

Deloria, Philip Joseph. *Playing Indian*. Yale Historical Publications. Yale University Press, 1998.

Denetdale, Jennifer Nez. "Chairmen, Presidents, and Princesses: The Navajo Nation, Gender, and the Politics of Tradition." *Wicazo Sa Review* 21, no. 1 (2006): 9–28, https://doi.org/10.1353/wic.2006.0004.

Fryberg, Stephanie A.; Hazel Rose Markus; Daphna Oyserman; and Joseph M. Stone. "Of Warrior Chiefs and Indian Princesses: The Psychological Consequences of American Indian Mascots." *Basic and Applied Social Psychology* 30, no. 3 (2008): 208–18, https://doi.org/10.1080/01973530802375003.

Kauanui, J. Kēhaulani. "'A Structure, Not an Event': Settler Colonialism and Enduring Indigeneity." *Lateral: Journal of the Cultural Studies Association*, Emergent Critical Analytics for Alternative Humanities, Issue 5.1 (Spring 2016), https://doi.org/10.25158/L5.1.7.

Kilpatrick, Jacquelyn. *Celluloid Indians: Native Americans and Film*. University of Nebraska Press, 1999.

Littletree, Sandra; Miranda Belarde-Lewis; and Marisa Duarte. "Centering Relationality: A Conceptual Model to Advance Indigenous Knowledge Organization Practices." *Knowledge Organization* 47, no. 5 (2020): 410–26, https://doi.org/10.5771/0943-7444-2020-5-410.

Moreton-Robinson, Aileen. "Relationality: A Key Presupposition of an Indigenous Social Research Paradigm." In *Sources and Methods in Indigenous Studies*, edited by Chris Anderson and Jean M. O'Brien. Routledge, 2017.

Pham, Vivian. "Finding Culture under Concrete: Urban Rez by Larissa FastHorse." Mapping Indigenous Los Angeles, UCLA (blog), September 20, 2016, https://mila.ss.ucla.edu/2016/09/20/finding-culture-concrete-urban-rez-larissa-fasthorse/.

Raheja, Michelle H. *Reservation Reelism: Redfacing, Visual Sovereignty, and Representations of Native Americans in Film*. University of Nebraska Press, 2010.

Ramos, Kenny. "*Urban Rez*: Native American Actor Kenneth Ramos on Representing Indigenous Communities." LinkTV. ArtBound (blog), March 25, 2016.

Rickard, Jolene; George Longfish; Zig Jackson; Pamela Shields Carroll; Ron Carraher; and Hulleah Tsinhnahjinnie. "Sovereignty: A Line in the Sand." *Aperture*, no. 139 (Summer 1995): 50–59, https://archive.aperture.org/article/1995/2/2/sovereignty-a-line-in-the-sand.

Rifkin, Mark. *When Did Indians Become Straight? Kinship, the History of Sexuality, and Native Sovereignty*. Oxford University Press, 2011.

Sepulveda, Charles. "Our Sacred Waters: Theorizing Kuuyam as a Decolonial Possibility." *Decolonization: Indigeneity, Education & Society* 7, no. 1: Indigenous Peoples and the Politics of Water (2018): 40–58.

Simpson, Audra. "Whither Settler Colonialism?" *Settler Colonial Studies* 6, no. 4 (2016): 438–45, https://doi.org/10.1080/2201473X.2015.1124427.

Speed, Shannon. "Structures of Settler Capitalism in Abya Yala." *American Quarterly* 69, no. 4 (2017): 783–90, https://doi.org/10.1353/aq.2017.0064.

"*Urban Rez* Shines Light on L.A.'s Indigenous People 'Declared Extinct' by Government." *The Frame, LAist.* 89.3 KPCC, April 26, 2016, https://www.scpr.org/programs/the-frame/2016/04/22/48214/larissa-fasthorses-idigenous-play-urban-rez/. [sic]

Wilson, Shawn. *Research Is Ceremony: Indigenous Research Methods.* Fernwood Publishing, 2008.

Wolfe, Patrick. "Settler Colonialism and the Elimination of the Native." *Journal of Genocide Research* 8, no. 4 (2006), https://doi.org/10.1080/14623520601056240.

URBAN REZ

Created through collaboration between Larissa FastHorse, Michael John Garcés, and Indigenous people of the Los Angeles Basin

PRODUCTION HISTORY

Urban Rez was commissioned, developed, and produced by Cornerstone Theater Company in Tovaangar from April 7–17, 2016, at the Los Angeles State Historic Park, and from April 21–May 1, 2016, at Kuruvungna Springs. The scenic design was by Shannon Scrofano, the costume design was by Meghan E. Healey, the lighting design was by Geoff Korf, and the sound design was by John Nobori. The production stage manager was Ash Nichols, the associate director was Daniel Penilla, and the assistant director was Jason Grasl. The cast was:

HELEN	Danielle Aguilar
XAVIER	Frank Ayala
ADRIENNE	Clementine Bordeaux
ANTOINE	Marcenus "M.C." Earl
WANDA	Sheri Foster
GOVERNMENT PERSON	Peter Howard
HAILEY	Kinsale Hueston
TASHA	Terri Jay
ROBIE	Jenny Marlowe
ED	Leland Morrill
BAHE	Maxine Napoleon
NEASHA	Cecelia Phoenix
MAX	Kenny Ramos
WALTER	Willie Sandoval
TONI	Arianna Taylor

Community partners for *Urban Rez* included the Red Circle Project, the Gabrielino-Tongva Springs Foundation at University High School, the UCLA American Indian Studies Department, Rancho Los Alamitos, and California State Parks.

THE FORMAT

Urban Rez is an immersive fair, blending fact and fiction. As participants (audience members) check in, they are given a shell sticker or a flag sticker. Participants should be told to keep their sticker on and encouraged to explore the fair, but not directed in any other way. For this experience, there is value in both agency and alienation.

The script is divided into Rounds, Stories, and Scenes. All Stories in Rounds 2–9 are performed in Scenes, which happen simultaneously during each Round in different locations of the performance space. During these Rounds, all booths in the Cultural Fair are active, and so there are unscripted, informal conversations and interactions between cast members and participants happening as well. This creates a sense of simultaneous action throughout the space. All Stories in Rounds 10 through 12 happen consecutively. Participants choose Scenes and Stories to engage with and cannot experience everything they want to.

THE CHARACTERS

Unless specified, any gender identity works for all characters. Any pronouns or gender-specific references should match the preferred pronoun of the actor. This script reflects the original cast.

MAX: Nicoleño, not an elder, good improviser with participants
ROBIE: Nicoleño, not an elder, female or male (Antoine has to be the opposite gender)
XAVIER: Native American from any tribe, elder, male

TEJON: Indian, joke teller, funny improvised banter
WANDA: Not Native, wannabe NDN
NEASHA: Nicoleño, elder, female
ANTOINE: Black, dating Robie, male or female (Robie has to be the opposite gender)
GOVERNMENT PERSON (GP): White, any age
TASHA: Native American, any age
TONI: Native American from a reservation, any age, trans MTF
BAHE: Nicoleño, any age
HELEN: Xicana, any age
ADRIENNE: Nicoleño, not an elder
WALTER: Nicoleño, any age
HAILEY: Nicoleño, teen
ED: Native American from federally recognized tribe, any age

NOTE

The Nicoleño people lived on San Nicolas Island but were killed by invaders or died from the diseases they brought with them. The Nicoleño were related to the Gabrielino/Tongva/Kizh people of Southern California.

THE URBAN REZ

An outdoor cultural fair divided into three main areas:

WELCOMING SPACE

This is a holding area where participants cannot observe the Communal Space or the Cultural Fair until they are given entrance. An area where there are platforms, booths, and undefined places where community members sell or share their art, food, crafts, or medicines. They share information about their organizations, perform music as inspired, dance together, or simply hold space for gathering. This is also where the Sign-In Booth is. At the Sign-In Booth, all participants are given a shell or flag sticker. For groups, one or two members are given a different sticker than the rest.

COMMUNAL SPACE

This is a circle or oval comprised of:

> THE STAGE: Community stage where Indigenous folks perform.
>
> THE SHARED CIRCLE: An open area where all performers and participants can gather to watch what is on the Stage or to circle up together.

THE CULTURAL FAIR

This is a group of booths arranged in a circle or oval facing into the center, with an entrance for people who are coming in from the Welcoming Space. It is concurrent with the Communal Space, so performers and participants can easily move from one to the other. They are different but not separate. There is a lot of room within the circle of booths for participants and performers to move from booth to booth. There are places for people to sit among the booths. There are also camp chairs for people to carry with them if they desire. The booths making up the Cultural Fair are:

> LIVE OFF THE LAND/NATIVE PLANTS MATTER: A biologist or trained person has samples of plants native to Southern California and teaches us what the different plants are used for.
>
> MAPPING THE AREA/GOOGLE MAPS 1491 (CA VERSION): The leader gets people to try to place the tribes in the correct locations of their original homelands on a map of L.A. and Orange Counties. After participants have made their attempt, the correct map of the original people of the counties is shared. Then the current federal government map, which has no tribes at all, is revealed.
>
> FEDERAL GOVERNMENT BOOTH: Government Person's hangout. All the government forms are kept here until they are deployed.
>
> DANCES WITH TIGER LILY: Two leaders have various costume pieces inspired by Hollywood Indian characters. Participants compete to dress up as the most stereotypical Indian. They can add wigs from different movies. The leaders pick

a winner, then tell which pieces are from actual tribes and which are made up. The booth is decorated with pictures of bad movie representations of Indians and actual Indians of the same tribes.

GREAT OPPORTUNITIES IN THE CITY/INDIAN RELOCATION ACT: Roving booth with pictures of relocated people. Leaders read stories of relocation, bad and good. The leaders tell participants about the huge Native population influx in L.A. due to relocation.

NDN 101: Leader plays various cultural games with participants: word-matching cards, which book doesn't belong, Tongva commands that become a dance, etc.

INSTANT KARMA/GUILT REDUCTION: The leader gives non-Native people a list of tasks to do during the fair. They must get them signed off and bring the list back to get a "certificate of reduced guilt."

DEFEND YOUR CULTURE: Participants learn the difference between appreciation and appropriation of Indigenous cultures by exploring topics like Columbus Day, feather headdresses, missions, etc. Participants are encouraged to identify things that are Native in origin that they wear or use in their daily life, and defend their choice to do so.

DANZA: Helen's hangout to educate and promote Mayan dance.

OTHERS: Other booths as suggested by cast and community members. An important one to the original production was the Red Circle Project Booth. The Red Circle Project, which ended operations on May 15, 2020, was the only HIV prevention program in L.A. County that provided service to American Indians and Alaska Natives. They were a key partner organization during the development and production of *Urban Rez*, and their booth had pamphlets, flyers, stickers, and a rainbow array of condoms. There were other booth spaces made available to community partners and allied service organizations, such as the Gabrielino-Tongva Springs Foundation, These Days Gallery, and Retention for American Indians Now! (RAIN!), who tabled and shared information.

PROLOGUE

EVERYONE

Cultural Fair

After spending time in the Welcoming Space, participants and performers are admitted into the Cultural Fair to check out booths, where they meet additional performers. All participants explore for ten minutes, playing the games and watching videos.

Since the booths in the Cultural Fair are already set up and the circle is full, Max, who was out in the Welcoming Space, is late to put out his table. Max sets up his booth in the Communal Space near the stage. Max puts out artwork with a sign: "Native American Art by Max Higuera, a Nicoleño Tribal Member of Southern California."

Eventually Xavier and Neasha grab mics to draw people to the Communal Space. Performers encourage participants to come with them.

ROUND ONE

EVERYONE

Communal Space

XAVIER: Welcome to Urban Rez! Just a couple announcements to kick things off. Neasha?

NEASHA: Thank you. The bathrooms and exits are back out the way you came in. There's lots of things to experience today. Choose something that sparks your fancy and see where it takes you. There's no right or wrong way to enjoy Urban Rez.

XAVIER: But do be sure to leave chairs for the elders. *(To Neasha)* That's for you, old woman.

NEASHA: I can run circles around you.

XAVIER: And she has. Let's start with a little creative writing from young Max and Robie to remind us why we need to meet like this. Max is quite the artist. Be sure to buy lots from his table over here. And Robie is . . . really a great girl. Always giving back.

MAX: Thanks Xavier.

ROBIE: Auntie Neasha.

MAX: Hunger for culture. I feel like I don't belong here, every day. The land is invisible. I am invisible. Our culture has been devoured and it feels like there is nothing left.
ROBIE: But then I remember that once there was a village at the beginning of the Harbor Freeway. The ancestors traveled those places that became roads. So when I drive on the freeway it is ancestor time. Time to remember the stories.
MAX: Time to get the courage to ask to hear the stories again
ROBIE: Hunger for culture, that's what Urban Rez is here to feed.
MAX: Ask. Listen. Investigate.
ROBIE: No matter who you are.
MAX: We create our own tribe today.
GOVERNMENT PERSON: With the understanding that only the federal government is empowered to recognize tribes as legitimate or not.
NEASHA: Who invited the federal government?
GOVERNMENT PERSON: The American government does not need to be invited. We're old friends.
NEASHA: Friends? You declared my tribe extinct!
GOVERNMENT PERSON: Oh, but we've done so much lovely paperwork together.
XAVIER: Because you returned every application they sent to be recognized as a tribe again.
GOVERNMENT PERSON: But we did recognize your tribe, Xavier, so you and I are officially pals.
XAVIER: Friends don't declare friends extinct in the first place.
NEASHA: You have erased us from our own lands, from the present moment, even from history.
GOVERNMENT PERSON: Not entirely, but . . .
BAHE: My tribe will be gone in three generations. What are you doing to help us?
GOVERNMENT PERSON: What is your definition of "help"?
TASHA: My tribe forced me out because of the system you put in place. What are you doing to fix that?
GOVERNMENT PERSON: It's up to each tribe to—

(The speed of the requests increases, everyone piling on with issues for the government.)

HAILEY: Young people are killing themselves on reservations every day. What are you doing to help them?
ED: What are you doing about adequate drinking water?
WALTER: What about intergenerational trauma?
HELEN: The ancestors on display in universities?
ANTOINE: How about reparations?
TONI: Institutional racism?
ADRIENNE: What about preserving our language?
XAVIER: What about honoring the treaties?
ROBIE: What are you doing to save our culture?
MAX: To protect our art?
NEASHA: What are you doing to help our tribe, Fed?
GOVERNMENT PERSON: What tribe? You have no tribe!
WANDA: They are the Nickelodeon—
ADRIENNE: It's Nicoleño!
WANDA: Nicoleño, and you saying they are extinct doesn't make it true. I am Nicoleño! I am Nicoleño!
OTHERS: I am Nicoleño! I am Nicoleño!
NEASHA: Today WE define who we are! You are not welcome here, Fed!

(The others advance on GP. He backs into Max's display. Max rushes over to protect his art.)

OTHERS *(Simultaneously)*: Get out! / You tell him! / Get rid of the fed! / Hit the road jack!
MAX: Watch it! That's my art.
GOVERNMENT PERSON: You are Max Higuera?
MAX: Yes.
GOVERNMENT PERSON: So this is your "Native American" art?
MAX: Yes.
GOVERNMENT PERSON: I demand to see your federally recognized enrollment card.

(The mood changes, confidence falters.)

MAX: Why?

GOVERNMENT PERSON: Because as a representative of the federal government I am sworn to uphold the Indian Arts and Crafts Act. Show me your card.

MAX: These are my tribal homelands.

GOVERNMENT PERSON: There are no federally recognized tribes in Los Angeles or Orange County. Which means that I will need to confiscate this work and detain you.

(Government Person knocks over the table and grabs Max. Chaos erupts.)

You brought this on yourselves. You asked the government to protect legitimate Native American artists from imposters and mass-produced goods that were sold as authentic. This is a federal matter now.

(GP gathers Max's art.)

MAX: A federal matter?
NEASHA: A federal matter?
XAVIER: A federal matter.
EVERYONE: A federal matter.

(A Federal Matter dance. Something that explores what those words mean to everyone: hurt, safety, confusion, authority, rebellion. It ends with three distinct groupings:
  GP, Max, Neasha, and Wanda.
  Xavier, Antoine, and Robie.
  Hailey, Ed, Walter, and Bahe.)

It's a federal matter. What can we do?

(The three groups overlap to the end of the scene as they move physically away from each other. As they interact they gradually move back into the Cultural Fair.)

NEASHA: How can I help my nephew?

XAVIER: You've got the guilt, I've got the cure.
HAILEY: We're setting the record straight.
GOVERNMENT PERSON: You can visit him in federal prison.
XAVIER: Xavier's Guilt Reduction Booth.
HAILEY: Appreciation or appropriation?
WANDA: I'll rally the tribe.
ROBIE: But I don't have guilt?
HAILEY: Ignorance is no excuse.
MAX: I don't need help from a wannabe.
XAVIER: Everyone has guilt.
ED: Educate not implicate.
NEASHA: If only there was a loophole.
XAVIER: A loophole for your guilt.
HAILEY: Learning but no loopholes.
GOVERNMENT PERSON: Did you say a loophole? This is the federal government. There's always a loophole. Come with me to the government booth and we'll talk.
NEASHA: Someone gave you a booth?
GOVERNMENT PERSON: I'm here to serve the Indians, ma'am.
HAILEY: We're setting the record straight. Come on.
XAVIER: You've got the guilt, I've got the cure. Follow me.

(As the participants follow the cast into the Cultural Fair, the following scenes erupt, along with spontaneous, unscripted conversations: Max Story—Scene 1 and Hailey Story—Scene 1.)

MAX STORY—SCENE I

Cultural Fair

Max, Neasha, and Government Person walk to GP's booth.

MAX: I do have an enrollment card issued from my tribe.
GOVERNMENT PERSON: But we've established that your tribe no longer exists.
MAX: Are you honestly going to say that I can't sell my artwork on my own ancestral lands?

NATIVE NATION PROJECT

GOVERNMENT PERSON: You cannot sell "Native American art" on any land. All of your "art" will be confiscated and destroyed after your trial.
MAX: This is how I make my living.
GOVERNMENT PERSON: Not anymore. Unless you are a member of a federally recognized tribe. I can make that happen.
NEASHA: Really?
MAX: Then I can sell my art?
GOVERNMENT PERSON: Of course.

(Government Person settles into his booth. He's at home, official.)

How may I help you?
MAX: Um, you're detaining me?
GOVERNMENT PERSON: And what can I do about it?
MAX: You just said we could clear all this up by getting recognition.
GOVERNMENT PERSON: And you are?
MAX: I am Nicoleño.
GOVERNMENT PERSON: Hello, Nicoleño.
MAX: That's not me, that's my tribe.
GOVERNMENT PERSON: I've never heard of it.
NEASHA: It's a tribe from the Los Angeles Basin. The islands originally.
GOVERNMENT PERSON: There are no tribes from the Los Angeles Basin.
NEASHA: There are.
GOVERNMENT PERSON: There aren't.
MAX: This again. How do we apply for recognition?

(Government Person pulls out a form. Max takes one and scans it.)

GOVERNMENT PERSON: This is the summary of "25 CFR Part 83: Procedures for Establishing that an American Indian Group Exists as an Indian Tribe: 83.7 Mandatory Criteria for Federal Acknowledgment." The full statement is fifteen pages long. The application timeline explanation is four pages long. The petition itself is quite involved. Once all of the procedures are followed and properly submitted, if all goes well you should have an answer in twenty to thirty years.

(Max laughs. Government Person doesn't.)

MAX: That's a joke right?
GOVERNMENT PERSON: Which part?
MAX: The twenty or thirty years.
GOVERNMENT PERSON: No. That's if all goes well.
MAX: Is a different part a joke?
GOVERNMENT PERSON: We don't joke. We're the federal government.
NEASHA: But it has to happen today.
GOVERNMENT PERSON: Why, do you need college grants?
MAX: I need to stay out of prison. And get my art back.
GOVERNMENT PERSON: Or perhaps health care? Because if you are a recognized tribe, you can get that.
NEASHA: Actually I have some issues. If doing this helps, that's good.
GOVERNMENT PERSON: You will probably want to hire an attorney and someone to trace your ancestry, a historian and an ethnographer. Perhaps a governmental consultant and a grant writer to fund all of this. Unless you have your own money.
MAX: We don't have anything.

(Government Person hands over a stack of forms.)

GOVERNMENT PERSON: And if you make one mistake or we find one error in one proposed tribal member, the entire application is rejected and you start over.
NEASHA: This is the same old story. You said you would help us.
GOVERNMENT PERSON: That's not entirely what the government is for.

(Max studies the papers. It's impossible. He leaves to figure it out.)

HAILEY STORY—SCENE I

Cultural Fair

Defend Your Culture Booth. Hailey gets set up in her booth and calls people over.

ED: Hailey, I'm so glad to see young people like yourself involved, but I think the tone we want today is inclusive.

HAILEY: Inclusive like when my school teams play the Chiefs and burn a papier-mâché Native American man on a bonfire?

ED: I'm sure that's upsetting.

HAILEY: Or when the Chiefs' fans do that "whoo whoo whoo" thing every time they score? That makes me feel really included.

ED: Those things are hurtful, but with age you learn that a gentler approach attracts more supporters.

HAILEY: I don't want to be disrespectful, Ed, but you have no idea what my life is like. You grew up on a reservation with Indians everywhere. I'm the ONLY Native American in my entire high school. So every time the Chiefs play or it's Columbus Day or we go to a mission or it's Halloween or we have a concert, I'm literally the only person in thousands who cares that what they are doing is hurtful.

ED: That's got to be hard.

HAILEY: I once saw a girl at a pow wow from a school we play all the time. I didn't know she was Native. I went up to her and she said no one knows. They all assume she's Mexican and she decided it was easier to learn Spanish than be alone. I swore that I'd never be that girl. When I leave my school, everyone will know that there was a Native American that graduated there and she made people think.

ED: OK, make me think.

(Hailey pulls up a PowerPoint of various folks improperly wearing headdresses.)

HAILEY: Let's start with an easy one. Feather headdresses. NO. Unless you earned every feather with proper ceremonies, you may never ever wear a headdress. Like this. Or this. Or Pharrell. Or Gwen Stefani. Or these Boy Scouts. And if you are hosting a concert or festival, you can ban them. Like they did at Osheaga or the Bass Coast Festival and lots of other Canadian music festivals. People still come, the music still sounds the same, and no one has to suffer the trauma of this. That's appropriating something sacred to another culture because you want it.

(She shows a particularly offensive festival picture. Then shows pictures of Native art using feathers or feather images.)

Here's some great feather accessories made by Native American artists that you can buy and wear because they are art, not culture. The artist for this piece, Ed, is right here. Buying from Native artists, that's appreciation of art from a specific culture and keeps those cultural arts alive so they can pass them on to the next generation. Right, Ed?

ED: Absolutely.

(Ed moves on as Hailey shows more slides.)

ROUND TWO

XAVIER STORY—SCENE I

Cultural Fair

From here forward, until indicated otherwise, all scenes in each Round happen simultaneously.
   Instant Karma/Guilt Reduction Booth. Xavier gathers folks, including Wanda. Antoine and Robie walk by.

XAVIER: Well, that was exciting. Step right up for some guilt reduction. That's you, white guy. Hey, you look guilty. Brothers are welcome; you're on our land too.
ANTOINE: Did you just say "brothers"? As in Black people?
WANDA: Are you on Indian land?
ANTOINE: Yes.
WANDA: Then you're guilty too.
ANTOINE: My ancestors were brought here in slave ships, you know.
WANDA: Then go home.
ANTOINE: Excuse me?
WANDA: Because right now you are in their home. You better act like it.

ANTOINE: I don't need to take this from a wannabe.

WANDA: I'm not a wannabe.

ROBIE: I'm a Nicoleño tribal member and Antoine is absolutely welcome in my home. You know, as a friend. As he would be welcome in any of our homes. If they know him or are friends, like me. We've got a booth to run.

(Antoine and Robie go.)

XAVIER: OK, emotions running high at Urban Rez. Politics, culture, and recognition, oh my!

WANDA: I can organize a rally. Or call the press. I've got protest signs in my car.

XAVIER: You carry protest signs around?

WANDA: Generic ones, just in case.

XAVIER: Thanks but I'll take it from here. *(To group)* OK, there's a lot to feel guilty about, my friends, and Xavier has the cure.

(Wanda goes past the Red Circle Project Booth to get her signs. Xavier continues gathering people with banter. Once a few are gathered:)

Hey everyone, I'm a Tejon Indian from California. I grew up with my people, on my lands. Next thing you want to know is if I'm a full blood. Nope, just came from the Red Cross so I'm a pint short. We're going to get you back some karma you lost because of your ancestors and all your white privilege and such. First I need you all to kneel and bow to me. Jokes. Jokes. Here's the deal. For this day only on Urban Rez you can work off that guilt in a few different ways. I've got a list for you. Go find a tree, peel off some bark to write on, make a pen out of twigs and charcoal, and write this down. I'm kidding. I've got it all printed up here on pure white paper, to make most of you comfortable. Anyway, get some of this list signed off, bring it back and I'll personally reduce your guilt. You get a certificate and everything. No joke. Though I know some good ones.

Before you go out there, I give you my top-five list of things to say to a white person:

1. My great-great-grandmother was a full-blooded white American princess.
2. Do you live in a covered wagon?
3. How much white are you?
4. What's the meaning behind the square dance?
5. Funny, you don't look white.

Think about it. Now go out there and work off that guilt. I'll be here waiting.
    Work off that guilt!

(Xavier sends them off. The tasks are in the appendix, p. 83. The first set is doable at Urban Rez and gets you one percent reduced guilt. The second set gives you the other ninety-nine percent but cannot be completed at the fair.)

WANDA STORY—SCENE I

Cultural Fair

The Red Circle Project Booth. As Wanda leaves she runs into Toni.

WANDA: Why won't they let me help them? If we're going to "create our own tribe today," shouldn't I be allowed to identify however I want?

TONI: Don't get me started.

WANDA: I probably know more about being Native than most of the people here. For sure more than that half-breed girl.

TONI: Don't say "half breed." It's nearly worse than saying "she-male."

WANDA: I'd love to be called a half breed. At least they would acknowledge me.

TONI: When I transitioned from Tony with a "Y" to Toni with an "I," I was still living on the rez and got my head bashed in with a cinder block. Trust me, being acknowledged there isn't always good.

WANDA: But don't most tribes consider Two-Spirit people sacred?

TONI: First, I don't identify as Two-Spirit, I'm all woman. Second, many of our people have been colonized, body, mind, and soul.

WANDA: So you don't ever visit your rez?

TONI: I'm still Native above all else, but I mostly just go back for funerals and babies.
WANDA: If I had a reservation that claimed me, I'd never leave. No matter what. Better to die part of something than live alone.
TONI: Are you even Native?
WANDA: Not that I can prove. But I've always felt it. Like I'm in the wrong skin.
TONI: Girl, I hear that.
WANDA: At least you know who you are.
TONI: If you worry about what others think of you, you'll drive yourself insane. Just be you and trust that that's enough.
WANDA: But it's not.

(Wanda continues on to the community services tables.)

ANTOINE/ROBIE STORY—SCENE I

Cultural Fair

Dances with Tiger Lily Booth. Antoine and Robie arrange things to give a presentation.

ANTOINE: Can you believe what she said to me?
ROBIE: Well, I'd believe just about anything people say. Should I have gone with Max and Neasha?
ANTOINE: There's nothing you can do.
ROBIE: I guess. I feel so helpless.
ANTOINE: Go check in with your family, Robie. I can handle this.
ROBIE: If I ran to my family every time there was drama, I'd never have a life.
ANTOINE: As long as there's drama already, maybe we should tell them about us today?
ROBIE: Are you crazy?
ANTOINE: I've never been clear on why we have to date in secret.
ROBIE: Because we're not just a family, we're a tribe. We're the last of an entire race of people. I want one thing in my life that is mine, not theirs.

ANTOINE: But if we keep dating, they'll know eventually, right?
ROBIE: In theory.
ANTOINE: Our relationship is both secret and theoretical?
ROBIE: Our relationship is good. Trust me, my family has a way of taking over your life.
ANTOINE: I'm pretty involved already. I mean I'm here working this Urban Rez thing with you. Don't you think it's becoming obvious why I'm here all the time?
ROBIE: They probably think you're a wannabe.
ANTOINE: You know my people and your people have been sheltering each other and intermarrying for centuries. I could be Native American.
ROBIE: I'm sorry I said that, but when it comes to dating and my family it's tricky. You don't identify as Native and . . . to be totally honest, not everyone would be OK with me dating a non-Native guy.
ANTOINE: Are you serious?
ROBIE: It's old-school thinking.
ANTOINE: Do you think like that?
ROBIE: At least you're not white, but . . .
ANTOINE: But what?
ROBIE: But why stir things up when we're just barely dating?
ANTOINE: It's been three months.
ROBIE: But secretly, so it's more like two.
ANTOINE: That makes no sense.
ROBIE: I'm a complicated woman.

(They lean in to kiss.)

ADRIENNE: Hey Robie.

(They pull away.)

ANTOINE: OK. We'll wait for now.
ADRIENNE: I need help heckling these people.
ANTOINE: Go. I'm fine.

(Robie goes with Adrienne.)

ROBIE: Did you hear about Max?

ADRIENNE: It's gonna bring our tribe together.

ANTOINE *(To participants)*: Who wants to compete to dress up as the most stereotypical Indian? The more wrong you are, the more likely you'll win.

ROUND THREE

MAX STORY—SCENE 2

Cultural Fair

Max finds GP.

MAX: But you said there is a loophole.
GOVERNMENT PERSON: Oh. You are asking for the loophole? Special treatment? From the government?
MAX: That's what you just said.
GOVERNMENT PERSON: Well, we are having a grace period amnesty filibuster lame duck shutdown magical application period for the Urban Rez today. If you can get your entire application filled out before the day ends and bring enough members to prove you are a legitimate tribal group, we'll grant you recognition now.
MAX: Right now? Not in thirty years?
GOVERNMENT PERSON: Only if you get it in today.
NEASHA: Then Max doesn't have to go to jail?
GOVERNMENT PERSON: There would be no reason.
NEASHA: And we'd get that health care and the education grants?

GOVERNMENT PERSON: Of course. Maybe even a casino.
NEASHA: We don't want a casino.
MAX: Well . . . we could think about it.
GOVERNMENT PERSON: Do that. But be careful, the same rules apply. If you try to enroll one false Indian, everyone is rejected. Do you understand?
MAX: I do.

(Max starts to go.)

GOVERNMENT PERSON: You've been detained.
NEASHA: We need every tribal member to make this happen. Including Max.
GOVERNMENT PERSON: I can't just set him free.
NEASHA: He won't leave the Urban Rez, you have my word.
GOVERNMENT PERSON: This could work for me. OK, but not one foot off the reservation.

(GP holds out his hand to Neasha. She shakes.)

ROUND FOUR

XAVIER STORY—SCENE 2

Cultural Fair

Instant Karma/Guilt Reduction Booth. Government Person passes.

XAVIER: Hey Fed, you wanna work off some guilt?
GOVERNMENT PERSON: Don't have any.
XAVIER: I believe that. How about you take one of these anyway? Think of the tasks as a game.
GOVERNMENT PERSON: I've got a game going already. A special game for government employees only.
XAVIER: So it's just you playing? Guess you're going to win.
GOVERNMENT PERSON: No, this game's been ongoing for hundreds of years. I'm just one in a long line of players, but I think my chances are pretty good today. I can at least get on the leaderboard.
XAVIER: Wow. What's this game called?
GOVERNMENT PERSON: The American Government Plan for Eradication (or Assimilation) of All Indigenous Peoples.
XAVIER: Catchy. Guess you don't want me on your team.

GOVERNMENT PERSON: Actually I get bonus points for turning a Native American person against another tribe as my scout. You wanna do that? You could keep an eye on those Lakota over there.
XAVIER: Naw. Bad eyes. I may get them mixed up with a Kickapoo and mess you up.
GOVERNMENT PERSON: It's not a game of accuracy.
XAVIER: I'm kinda busy anyway. Hey, Fed says "nepwaan."
GOVERNMENT PERSON: Nepwaan?
XAVIER: It's how the Nicoleño say "head." You just earned a point in my game. Sure you don't want to switch?
GOVERNMENT PERSON: Wait, I just met Nicoleño. Weird.

(He goes as Xavier turns back to his tasks.)

MAX STORY—SCENE 3

Cultural Fair

Mapping the Area/Google Maps 1491 (CA Version) Booth. A large map of Southern California and pieces labeled with each tribe from the area.

TASHA: Try to place the right tribe on the proper location in L.A. County and the OC. It's not a test, work together. Give it a try and see how many you get right.

(Max and Neasha walk by.)

MAX: Wait, you don't even have the Nicoleño on here.
TASHA: Who?
MAX: The survivors of our Island were moved to San Gabriel Mission.
TASHA: Look, it's not up to me to say who exists and who doesn't but ever since casinos came on the scene, there's some shady stuff going on with tribes.
NEASHA: We've always been here, and we don't want a casino.
TASHA: You do realize a gaming tribe in Los Angeles would be the wealthiest people in the nation? Billionaires.
MAX: No. Really? Billions!

TASHA: There it is, shade. Stay away from this whole thing, or before it's over you'll be kicking out grandma here to make more money.
MAX: I'd never do that.
NEASHA: I'm not his grandma.
TASHA: My ancestors have been Chukchansi as long as anyone can remember. Then the tribe wanted a casino. My family opposed it and all of us were kicked out. After thousands of years, we're tribeless.
MAX: If you were treated like that by your tribe, why are you still helping out?
TASHA: Because no matter what a piece of paper tells me, I'm still Native American.
NEASHA: I feel the same way. But the government isn't giving us a choice.
TASHA: Don't trust them.
MAX: We have to.

(Tasha continues mapping with participants.)

ANTOINE/ROBIE STORY—SCENE 2

Cultural Fair

Defend Your Culture Booth. Robie and Adrienne arrive at the booth.

ROBIE: You're gonna be with who you love, right?
ADRIENNE: Of course. It's not the 1800s.
ROBIE: Even if that person isn't Native.
ADRIENNE: Oh, no. I'd never be with a non-Native guy. I couldn't even date out of our tribe.
ROBIE: Seriously?
ADRIENNE: Think about it. If mixed breeds like us get with less-mixed people and have kids with them, those kids will be more Native than us, biologically speaking. Then if our kids get with less-mixed people and on and on, we could have a ton of full-blood Indians again if we follow the plan.
ROBIE: I don't think it works like that.
ADRIENNE: Careful baby-making brought back the Mohegans.

ROBIE: They don't even use blood quantum.
ADRIENNE: All I know is that they weren't a tribe, now they are. And they're rich. They followed a plan.
ROBIE: But it's not the 1800s. People fall in love.
ADRIENNE: If you raise your kids right, they fall in love with the right kind of person. It's our duty to our people to keep the tribe strong.
ROBIE: But language and culture, that's what makes us who we are. As long as we raise our kids with that, we're fine, no matter how mixed they are.
ADRIENNE: Well, we've only got like ten words left in our language so being Nicoleño has to mean more than that. If you have to, date whoever you want, just don't have kids with them.
ROBIE: Does everyone feel that way?
ADRIENNE: Everyone likes him but . . . we're ancestors in training. You have to think about the future of the people. Come on, let's take these guys down.

(Adrienne, Robie, and Hailey challenge the participants on their Native knowledge.)

ADRIENNE, ROBIE, AND HAILEY: How do you say "bird" in your language? Teach me to say good morning. How do you say "dolphin"? What did your people eat? What's your Indian name? How do you say "computer"? Don't you speak your language? Is anyone in your tribe fluent? How much of your culture survived the missions, really? Are you just making this up? Fake! You're not real Indians. Real Indians know their culture and language. You're a fraud! Get out of here! No land for you! Go! Now!

HAILEY STORY—SCENE 2

Cultural Fair

Defend Your Culture Booth. Hailey addresses participants.

HAILEY: Columbus Day. Celebration of a guy who got lost and instantly enslaved or killed all the people he ran in to. Seriously, how are we still celebrating this?

Thanksgiving is more complicated. It's sold as a positive Indian thing during Native American Heritage Month, but then we stick cut-out feathers on kids' heads and the pilgrims end up looking like decent people. The truth is that when the pilgrims and their shipmates landed, they instantly stole all the corn a village had stored for the winter. They also dug up a graveyard and robbed the bodies. They wrote about it and then wondered why the local people weren't so friendly to them. This after the Native peoples had already been attacked and decimated by diseases from previous ships. Despite all that, some Native people did feel sorry for the white people because they were dying like flies, so they taught them how to eat what was already here, duh, and kept them alive. Those same pilgrims later attacked a village and killed hundreds of men, women, and children, then brought the heads of those people home as trophies of victory. One story says that they kicked the heads down the street as a game and that's the actual first Thanksgiving celebration. Think about that while you gobble down your turkey.

ROUND FIVE

MAX STORY—SCENE 4

Cultural Fair

Live off the Land/Native Plants Matter Booth. Bahe tends to her plants.

BAHE: When I was a kid my father used to take us hunting for deer right in El Monte. They won't let you hunt in the middle of the city today, but the plants are still here for us.

(Max and Neasha find a place to sit and look over papers.)

MAX: Do you think that's true?
BAHE: Yes.
NEASHA: Native plants can give us nearly everything we need.
BAHE: I'd like to share some of those plants with you today.

(Bahe passes out samples of plants to the audience.)

MAX: No, the casino. The billions?
NEASHA: It can't be.

MAX: I guess. OK, you know our whole family tree, right?
NEASHA: I do.
MAX: We need the papers to trace that.
NEASHA: No papers. It's all in here. *(Taps head)*
MAX: There have to be papers.
NEASHA: For you and your parents. Maybe even some of your grandparents, but I was born on a ranch up in the San Gabriel Mountains. There were no papers then.
MAX: Something proved you belonged to your parents.
NEASHA: Bahe, you have your birth certificate?
BAHE: Never had one.
NEASHA: See? Our family Bible was the only place I was recorded. Used it to get my passport.
MAX: The government accepted the Bible as proof?
NEASHA: Yes.
MAX: Well then, I need that Bible.
NEASHA: It burned in the fire last year.
MAX: You're the key to this whole thing. You heard Tasha say we'd be the richest people in the nation. That's crazy.
NEASHA: Crazy's the right word.
MAX: Imagine the house you could buy with that money.
NEASHA: I think a billion is stretching it, but I do love me some bingo.
BAHE: Bingo!
MAX: If you're a billionaire you can have your own bingo hall. But first we need to work with the government to prove who we are.
NEASHA: You prove it by the way you live.
MAX: I know, but the government won't accept that as proof. Auntie, we have nothing. Nothing but ourselves. We've been this way since the first Europeans landed here. Nothing has changed for us in all of that time. I want what this government promised to us generations ago. And to keep me out of jail.
NEASHA: And to get rich?
MAX: We can use that money to change the world, not just for our tribe but for all the unrecognized tribes in California. We'll take care of our own.
NEASHA: Fine. What do you need me to do?
MAX: Start filling out the family tree. But we're going to need more help to prove all of this.

(Max goes. Neasha starts writing.)

WANDA STORY—SCENE 2

Cultural Fair

Wanda grabs Tasha and Toni.

WANDA: I've got it, girls! I called both of you here because I think we should be prepared for our response to the Government Person and a possible rally.
TONI: What are we responding to?
WANDA: The thing that happened with the artist. It isn't over.
TONI: I'm enrolled honey. I can sell anything I want.
TASHA: And I'm not an artist or technically Native anymore so I don't see what I can do.
WANDA: It's our responsibility as fellow activists to stand up and speak for the Nicoleño.
TASHA: Our responsibility? But none of us are Nicoleño.
WANDA: This situation gives us a chance to have a platform and be heard. We should take advantage of it. I'd like us to work up a statement in support of the Nicoleño that also encompasses our personal issues.
TONI: You want to work on transgender issues?
WANDA: Yes.
TASHA: The Nicoleño don't even have an enrollment yet and you want to talk about my disenrollment?
WANDA: This is a moment I think we should seize. I may be able to get some press here.
TONI: What are your issues, Wanda?
WANDA: I'm a conduit to serve my fellow humans. I feel like my place has always been to bring voices together and lift them up.
TASHA: First, I don't need my voice lifted. Second, this thing is called Urban Rez. It's about all Indian-identifying people in this city. I'm here to support that voice today.
WANDA: By joining together, as fellow outsiders, we can give better support.

TASHA: I'm not an outsider. I know exactly who I am.

(Tasha goes.)

WANDA: I'm just trying to help.
TONI: Look, I appreciate that you want to help. But it's not really your place to speak for them or anyone.
WANDA: But I'm an ally.
TONI: You know who was my strongest ally back home with my tribe?
WANDA: Who?
TONI: My grandmother.
WANDA: She stood up for you?
TONI: Nope. I don't think she's ever heard of "trans" anything. But she still taught me how to cook and called me when she needed someone to take her to the store. She knitted me scarves and spoke to me in our language. She didn't do anything except be herself and let me be me. That meant more to me than anything.
WANDA: But I need to do something.
TONI: Be of service. I'm sure someone would love to have you join their team.
WANDA: Fine. But I'm still writing a statement. Just in case.
TONI: You do that. I've got work to do.

HAILEY STORY—SCENE 3

Cultural Fair

Robie joins Hailey at the Defend Your Culture Booth.

ROBIE: Hailey, stay close. We may need to help out with this Max situation.
HAILEY: The perfect one is in danger, everyone panic!
ROBIE: He is our cousin. And the federal government is no joke.
HAILEY: The family won't let anything happen to the chosen one.
ROBIE: We should be ready to do . . . something.
HAILEY: I thought you were working with your man all day.
ROBIE: What man?

HAILEY: Antoine?

ROBIE: He's not my man. He's a man and we were working together because we are friends.

HAILEY: O. K.

ROBIE: So tell me about appropriation.

HAILEY: Well, it turns out I have this nifty video starring my very own cousin that talks about offensive Halloween costumes. She's a great girl.

(Hailey plays the video.)

ROUND SIX

MAX STORY—SCENE 5

Cultural Fair

While walking around, GP spots Max as he looks for help with the forms.

GOVERNMENT PERSON: How is it going, Nicoleño?
MAX: Fine, thanks. Do you need something?
GOVERNMENT PERSON: Just out checking tribal ID's. Making sure you are the only illegitimate Indian here. Have you thought about how you are going to define membership?
MAX: Well, everyone in our family. And everyone Auntie Neasha can trace back.
GOVERNMENT PERSON: So everyone is an equal member? Even if they are distant cousins? Is that fair?
MAX: I guess. There are unequal members?
GOVERNMENT PERSON: We put the blood quantum idea in place for a reason. What if you get a casino? Then people will come out of the woodwork to join. I'd advise you look at this blood quantum system. It's designed to keep the tribes strong.

(He holds up a blood quantum chart.)

MAX: I'll look at it.

GOVERNMENT PERSON: It's for the good of the tribe.

XAVIER STORY—SCENE 3

Cultural Fair

Instant Karma/Guilt Reduction Booth. Xavier address participants.

XAVIER: Just before Custer got ready to go into battle, he lined up all the bureaucrats from the Bureau of Indian Affairs and gave them express orders not to do anything until he returned. They have been following those orders ever since.

Two white guys and a Native American stand on top of a tall building. The first white guy says, "This is for my people!" and jumps. The second white guys says, "That doesn't make any sense." The Native guy thinks, then says, "Oh I get it. This is for my people!" and pushes the white guy off.

Why did white men go to the moon? They thought Indians owned land up there too.

When the US government wrote up the treaties with our people, we should have read the small print. It said, "This treaty is in effect as long as the grass grows and the river flows. Or ninety days, whichever comes first."

Why do Native Americans hate snow? Because it's white and settles on their land.

What's the difference between a fed and a snake? One is an evil, cold-blooded, venomous creature. The other is a snake.

GOVERNMENT PERSON: Xavier, can I see your CDIB please?

(Xavier gives GP his card. GP studies it, then hands it back and goes.)

XAVIER: What did the Indians call America before the white man came? Ours.

ROUND SEVEN

MAX STORY—SCENE 6

Cultural Fair

Dances with Tiger Lily Booth. Antoine and Robie help people put together a stereotypical Indian. Antoine puts a crazy getup on Robie.

MAX: Robie, I need your help filling out these forms. By the end of the day we'll be official Indians and can sell whatever we want and get benefits.

ROBIE: We're real Indians now, we always will be.

MAX: We both know that's not enough. But according to this, even if we get recognition, because your side of the family kept marrying out of the tribe, you'll be the last one of your line to be allowed in.

ROBIE: What do you mean?

MAX: You've got the minimum amount of Indian blood we can allow. Says so on the chart. The only way your kids get in is if you marry someone in the tribe, up their blood quantum.

ANTOINE: That sounds racist.

MAX: It's biology. According to the chart, a cousin would be best.

ROBIE: I'm not going to have kids with my cousin for their DNA.

MAX: It could be a distant cousin.
ROBIE: I'm not talking about this, Max.
MAX: Then your tribal line will stop with you.
ROBIE: I know you usually get away with anything, but the tribe won't let you take benefits away from my kids.
MAX: No casino money either.
ROBIE: What casino money?
MAX: From the one we'll build when we're recognized.
ROBIE: No one in the family has ever mentioned a casino.
MAX: We'll be billionaires. Billions. Trust me, they will want it. However, there has to be a cutoff. We're going to propose a standard blood quantum. Lots of tribes use it.
ROBIE: We who?
MAX: Everyone. Seriously, read the chart.
ROBIE: I don't need a chart to tell me that the concept of blood quantum was imposed on us by the conquerors to make sure we die out eventually. Don't be a part of their plan cousin.
MAX: Our genetics are preserved through blood quantum. And unique genetics are what make us valuable to the human race.
ROBIE: I thought it was our culture.
MAX: In today's world, we need both. It's your choice to carry on the tribe or not. Think about it.

(Max goes. Robie and Antoine exchange a look.)

WANDA STORY—SCENE 3

Cultural Fair

Danza Booth. Wanda approaches Helen with a "booth relief" sign.

WANDA: You need relief?
HELEN: Sure.
WANDA: Really? I'm Wanda.
HELEN: Helen. I'd love to take a break and run to the bathroom.
WANDA: I can stay all day.
HELEN: Isn't booth relief supposed to be for everyone?

WANDA: That's OK, I'd love to help you. What do you do?
HELEN: I'm here representing my dance group.

(Wanda brightens.)

WANDA: Pow wow?
HELEN: No, we do traditional Mayan dances.
WANDA: So I'm looking to sign up Mayan people? How do I know which ones they are?
HELEN: Anyone is welcome to our classes. You could come.
WANDA: I dance pow wow.
HELEN: Great. You're Native American?
WANDA: That's how I live my life.
HELEN: OK. So, just hand out flyers and if they have questions I'll be right back.
WANDA: You should teach me a sample class so people know what they're getting in to. I'll make you look good.

(Helen sits down.)

I thought you had to go?
HELEN: Not anymore. Maybe someone else needs relief?
WANDA: They don't want it from me even though I wrote this statement to support the artist guy and the Nicoleños and this transgender lady and another woman who got kicked out of her tribe. I thought it would help but . . . no one wants to read it.
HELEN: I'll read it.
WANDA: Really?
HELEN: Sure, as soon as I get back from the bathroom.
WANDA: Happy to be of service!

(Helen goes quickly as Wanda picks up pamphlets to read.)

XAVIER STORY—SCENE 4

Cultural Fair

As participants return to the Instant Karma/Guilt Reduction Booth, Xavier goes through their list, tells them more jokes, and gives them a "certificate of a percentage of reduced guilt" depending on how much they did. Then he hands out the second list (see appendix, p. 84). Sample jokes:

XAVIER: What does the mother buffalo say to her boy buffalo when she sends him off to college? Bye-son. Get it? Like bison. Like buffaloes? Aye!

Since this is California, what do you call a Lakota walking a dog? Vegetarian.

What do you call a Cheyenne walking two dogs? Rancher.

How do Indians know when it's safe to go ice fishing? When all the white guys quit falling through.

You know you're a twinkie if your spirit guide only speaks English.

You know you're a twinkie if roadkill makes you go, "Ew!" instead of, "Hey, new regalia!"

If Santa was an NDN, his new moccasins would be made out of Dasher and every tree would have a five-pound block of cheese and day-old bread underneath.

Where is the most dangerous place to be? Between me and my fry bread!

HAILEY STORY—SCENE 4

Cultural Fair

Adrienne joins Hailey at the Defend Your Culture Booth.

ADRIENNE: Did you hear about Max getting arrested? They took him to jail.

HAILEY: He's right over there.

ADRIENNE: Oh. I heard there was some loophole thing going on.

HAILEY: Whatever. I'm so sick of all this fighting in the tribe. We can't talk to Cesar's family because they applied without us once and they won't talk to us because of something stupid.

ADRIENNE: Yeah. Except Cesar's family is totally wrong.

HAILEY: About what?

ADRIENNE: Everything. Did you see the outfits they wore to that Chumash Day Pow Wow? They were made out of chamois from the auto-parts store.

HAILEY: But aren't chamois leather?

ADRIENNE: Yeah, but they could have gotten actual hides. People in L.A. don't even know we exist, so we have to be more authentic than normal. We can't do pow wow dances in bright colors like everyone else. We need to dress in our traditions and prove who we are.

HAILEY: But I dance fancy shawl. In colors.

ADRIENNE: You're actually appropriating another Native culture by doing fancy shawl. Do you want to be an appropriator?

HAILEY: But fancy shawl doesn't really belong to one specific tribe.

ADRIENNE: Look, we're not pow wow people in the first place so I'm not sure you should be there at all.

HAILEY: But lots of our family does pow wow.

ADRIENNE: Like Cesar.

HAILEY: You guys complain that not enough of young people come to these things, but this is why. We've got bigger issues to deal with. Have you seen the logo for the Washington Redskins? Or the big-nosed Cleveland Indian? We can't take care of these national issues if we're always fighting each other.

ADRIENNE: We deserve to be recognized. This is how we define who we are to the world.

(Adrienne goes.)

HAILEY: I'm just me and I'm Nicoleño. Nothing can change that.

ROUND EIGHT

HAILEY STORY—SCENE 5

Cultural Fair

The following three monologues happen at once at their various booths.

   (Defend Your Culture Booth:)

HAILEY: The missions. The Spanish conversion system was built on slavery and genocide. Auntie Neasha and Auntie Bahe are going to tell us some true stories. Since we're forced to represent missions in school, I thought we could learn ways to make our representations more accurate.

   (Live off the Land/Native Plants Matter Booth:)

BAHE: After the Russians attacked our Island to harvest all the sea otters for their pelts, the remaining people were moved to San Gabriel Mission. If you go there, you will see a well that is marked with a cross. The history you are told in schools is that six thousand Native people died from smallpox and were buried there. The truth is the Native people, our people, revolted against their enslavement by the Spanish. But they were slaughtered by the soldiers. Six thousand bodies were dumped in that well to cover up what the Spanish military had done to end the revolt. They still lie in that mass grave today.

(NDN 101 Booth:)

NEASHA: In 1785 at Mission San Gabriel, a twenty-five-year-old woman, Toypurina, was approached by a baptized captive, Nicolás José. Tired of the atrocities being committed by the Spanish invasion against the Gabrielinos, Nicolás José knew that Toypurina was highly respected by her people. Some say she was a medicine woman, others compare her to Joan of Arc because she had visions for her people. Either way, Nicolás José believed in Toypurina. She took up his challenge and organized a revolt of armed warriors. On October 25th, this young woman led the attack on the mission, but they had been betrayed and the Spanish military ambushed the Natives. The Spanish captured Toypurina and many of her warriors were jailed. The governor of Alta California, Pedro Fages, passed judgment at her trial. Toypurina's punishment was to be baptized and forced to leave her husband so she could be married to a Spanish soldier. She had to leave her people to move with him to Mission San Juan Bautista, where she eventually died.

WALTER STORY—SCENE I

Cultural Fair

Great Opportunities in the City/Indian Relocation Act Booth. During a space of silence, Walter rolls his booth in and addresses everyone.

WALTER: Indian Relocation Programs. These programs enticed Native people to leave their reservations and move to urban centers. Some people did well, but many became assimilated and lost touch with their Native cultures. Or never became assimilated and struggled. These are two of their stories.

My parents were both relocated to Los Angeles. My mom came with her family when she was a teen. She remembered that the government placed them in a hotel in downtown L.A. on Figueroa Street and gave them vouchers to pay their rent. After several weeks the family was moved to the Valley, where they had found a job for her father. They didn't see the government people again.

My dad went to Intermountain Inter-Tribal Boarding School when he was thirteen. They didn't bother educating him but did teach him to be a welder. As soon as he graduated he came with his cousins to L.A. as part of the relocation program. He got a job as a welder for the City of Santa Monica and worked there thirty years.

My parents met outside a bar in downtown L.A. My mom never went in, but she and her friends would hang out across the street from the bar where all the Indians went, and she met my dad there after the bar closed. They got married, had kids, and stayed in L.A.

My older cousin from Lower Brule was working odd jobs with a new wife and baby to support. He went to BIA and applied for a relocation program. They would send him to a city, but he had to complete a job-training program. He did it and became a plumber in the city. But he and his family were lonesome for home. They came back to take care of his ailing grandfather, but he couldn't get any decent jobs as a plumber so he went back to the BIA. They said he could go to another city if he went to training again. So off they went to a new place and he became a carpenter. But soon they were lonely for home. They went back for a visit then applied for another round of training in a new city. Eventually he became a plumber, carpenter, painter, electrician, auto mechanic, electronics repairman, and a few others I don't remember, and saw the whole country. In the end he came home and used all his skills to help his people. To this day he says, "It wasn't 'relocation,' it was 're-vacation'!"

MAX STORY—SCENE 7

Cultural Fair

Max sits at a table and works furiously.
 As other characters have time, they help out. Participants are asked to copy information onto forms.
 As he works, Max gets more and more desperate. It seems impossible.

ROUND NINE

ANTOINE/ROBIE STORY—SCENE 3

Cultural Fair

Dances with Tiger Lily Booth. Antoine and Robie look at each other.

ANTOINE: Max honestly wants you to think about marrying a cousin for their DNA? Yeah right.
ROBIE: Well . . . I probably should. At least a little.
ANTOINE: Are you kidding me?
ROBIE: Not a cousin, but tribes are allowed to set their own enrollment. I am mixed and although I identify as Nicoleño, biology is biology.
ANTOINE: Just because your cousin says our kids don't meet the minimum for enrollment doesn't mean they aren't Indian.
ROBIE: OUR kids? We've been secretly dating for the equivalent of two months.
ANTOINE: It's three.
ROBIE: Our ancestors were forced to hide being Nicoleño for so long. There's a lot of pressure on our generation to be out and proud.
ANTOINE: I'm fine with being proud of who you are, but I want a lot of kids.

ROBIE: So do I.

ANTOINE: But with me?

ROBIE: Three months!

ANTOINE: I'm not someone who likes to waste time. If there's no future, what's the point?

ROBIE: The point is, I care about you but . . . this affects my future children.

ANTOINE: How? I have health insurance from my job. You don't need their benefits.

ROBIE: It's not about health care. Enrollment makes my kids legitimate. Visible.

ANTOINE: You just told Max that being Native is about culture, not a piece of paper.

ROBIE: I believe that, but I also know what it's like to be invisible in my own home. Millions of people have invaded MY homeland and they don't even know I exist. We walked around nearly naked and lived in tule huts and had boats that sailed the ocean, but no one wants to see that. They want headdresses and teepees.

ANTOINE: That's why we're doing this Urban Rez thing. To show them who you are, without the naked part.

ROBIE: It's not enough. This won't change my everyday life. People will still talk to me in Spanish. The white people will be confused that I don't speak it and the Latinos will be mad at me. If my kids could have a chance to be real tribal members, shouldn't I give them that shot? Or should I let them be invisible to everyone, even their own tribe?

ANTOINE: You would honestly throw away what we have because I'm the wrong color?

ROBIE: Don't say it like that.

ANTOINE: That's what it is. It's racial engineering. It's Hit—

ROBIE: Don't say something you can't take back Antoine.

ANTOINE: You did.

ROBIE: I'm not deciding anything.

ANTOINE: But you are considering it. You are considering DNA over love.

ROBIE: Love. Please, try to understand. My ancestors had to survive slaughter, disease, slavery, a bounty on their heads, and boarding schools to bring this DNA to me. They hid who they were, took

Mexican names and did their ceremonies in secret to keep this culture alive. That's real love. Who am I to throw that love away?
ANTOINE: I hear you, but it's wrong. It has to be. If it isn't, then why can't white people only marry white people and black people only marry black people and on and on?
ROBIE: They can. It's their choice. Your choice. This one is mine.
ANTOINE: I can't believe you said that.

(Antoine goes.)

ROBIE: Wait. Come back!

WANDA STORY—SCENE 4

Cultural Fair

Danza Booth. Wanda chats with Helen.

WANDA: Isn't it ironic that people who don't have reservations, the original people of L.A. for instance, are doing this reservation-themed thing?
HELEN: Have you lived on a reservation?
WANDA: No. I grew up in L.A., but I've visited a lot. For sundance, pow wow. You know.
HELEN: Well, it's just a conceptual reservation.
WANDA: Real reservations are prisons. They are the sucky land that no one wanted.
HELEN: I am familiar with the concept.
WANDA: You know I heard most of these Southern California Indians are Mexican. Like mostly Mexican.
HELEN: I'm Mexican.
WANDA: Helen doesn't sound Mexican.
HELEN: I'm first generation here in California.
WANDA: Nothing against Mexicans, but that doesn't make you Indians.
HELEN: I'm Mayan, remember? And most Mexicans are part, if not fully, Indigenous.
WANDA: It's cool that you're a South American Indian but on this continent—

HELEN: Mexico is in North America.
WANDA: Are you sure?
HELEN: Yep. Yeah. Yes. I'm a North American Indian, Tzeltal.
WANDA: I thought you said Mayan. If this is supposed to be a rez, where's the commod cheese and the fry bread? Aa-yee.
HELEN: Fried bread and cheese aren't exactly Indigenous. To anywhere.
WANDA: I'm kidding. Although I really could use some fry bread. Where are the Navajos? Gather Indians together and there's always a Navajo selling fry bread, right? Whoolay.
HELEN: What does that mean?
WANDA: It's a Native American thing, you wouldn't understand.
HELEN: If you like reservations so much, why don't you live on one?
WANDA: I'm not enrolled anywhere so I can't live on reservation land. But I've always identified as Indian.
HELEN: Are you?
WANDA: I feel like I am. And I heard a rumor once about my great-great-grandmother Wanda being half Native. But she hid it because it was dangerous to be an Indian then.
HELEN: Sure.
WANDA: So I can't ever be enrolled, but these are my people. I feel it.
HELEN: I get that.
WANDA: Really?
HELEN: Everyone wants to belong somewhere. Be a part of something bigger than themselves.
WANDA: You know, people call me a twinkie.
HELEN: That doesn't sound good.
WANDA: It's not.
HELEN: I heard that artist guy's getting a tribe recognized here, today.
WANDA: Yeah. He's not very nice.
HELEN: I also heard they're letting people in.
WANDA: They could adopt me or something? Make me legit?
HELEN: I'd check it out.
WANDA: Are you going to join?
HELEN: It's not for me. I'm Xicana with an X. I like that.
WANDA: I guess I can ask.

(Wanda goes.)

ROUND TEN

XAVIER STORY—SCENE 5

Cultural Fair

From here forward, scenes are no longer simultaneous but consecutive. GP and Xavier spot each other across the space. They move together during the scene, a standoff.

XAVIER: Hey Fed, I heard you're passing out blankets.
GOVERNMENT PERSON: No, but that's a good idea. I could rack up some points.
XAVIER: Your game's not going so well?

(GP surveys the other scenes.)

GOVERNMENT PERSON: I wouldn't say that.
XAVIER: Sorry to hear it.
GOVERNMENT PERSON: You know, Xavier, now that we are officially connected by treaties, I think you should be more respectful of our relationship.

XAVIER: I was thinking the same thing about you.

GOVERNMENT PERSON: Hmm. Maybe we should draw up a new treaty to outline our expectations for each other.

XAVIER: I'll stick with the old treaties you aren't living up to. Why complicate things?

GOVERNMENT PERSON: I hear you there. While there are interesting contemporary developments—Cobell payments—oil pipelines, I've always been a fan of the classics.

XAVIER: Me too.

GOVERNMENT PERSON: Boarding school.

XAVIER: Alcatraz Occupation.

GOVERNMENT PERSON: Trail of Tears.

XAVIER: Battle of Little Big Horn.

GOVERNMENT PERSON: Wounded Knee 1890.

XAVIER: Wounded Knee 1973.

GOVERNMENT PERSON: This is an uncomfortable conversation.

XAVIER: We certainly don't want you to not be uncomfortable. Hey, I think I just saw someone trying to use an extra loophole over there.

(GP goes to investigate.)

WALTER STORY—SCENE 2

Cultural Fair

Great Opportunities in the City/Indian Relocation Act Booth. Walter and Hailey speak at the same time.

WALTER: Due to government relocation, Los Angeles County has the highest density of urban Indians than any other region. Some who came struggled. Some returned to their reservations. But others used the program to benefit themselves and their families. The children of relocation continue to adapt and thrive, making L.A. one of the most vibrant centers of Native American art and culture in the nation.

HAILEY STORY—SCENE 6

Cultural Fair

Defend Your Culture Booth.

HAILEY: It's estimated that during the Spanish Mission period more than sixty-two thousand Native people died at the missions. Some Native people fought back against the Spanish. A few won their lands back and some kept the military busy while their people fled. Those who survived suffered cruel punishments encouraged through the letters of Father Junípero Serra. The strength of those ancestors is our legacy.

ROUND ELEVEN

EVERYONE

Cultural Fair

The cast is spread through the space in pairs. They ask questions of participants and start small group chats. During this time they gently transition the participants from the Cultural Fair to the Communal Space.

Each pair starts with a question below, then lets the conversation flow.

ROBIE AND TASHA: What do you do to make sure your kids know their culture?
ANTOINE AND TONI: What makes you who you are, biology or choice?
HAILEY AND ED: If this was done to your people, could you forgive it?
WALTER AND HELEN: What place do you call home and why?
XAVIER AND NEASHA: What's making you uncomfortable today?
WANDA AND ADRIENNE: Would you become something you're not?
MAX AND BAHE: How far back do you know your family tree?

(Xavier calls people over to the stage for the Community Performance.

This is a non-curated space for Native American community members to perform something family-friendly for five to ten minutes.

Performances included ceremony, traditional dance, music, hip-hop dance, stand-up comedy, storytelling, etc. Sometimes the performances happen on the stage, but perhaps in the Shared Circle, with the performers helping to organize the participants around the Community Performance.)

XAVIER: It's time for a performance from our Indigenous community. Circle up everyone. Get close and get comfortable, four to a bench. Say hi to your neighbor. For you anti-social types, there are stools along the walls. Make a circle and settle in now.

Tonight our special guest is *(Name of performer[s])*.
And they will be sharing *(Type of performance)*.
Let's welcome them to Urban Rez!

(At the end, if the participants are standing in the Communal Space looking at the stage, the performers gently help organize the participants into a large circle facing in toward the center of the Communal Space. If they have already made that circle for the Community Performance, then the next scene can start immediately.)

ROUND TWELVE

ANTOINE/ROBIE STORY—SCENE 4

Communal Space

The rest of the scenes happen consecutively within the Shared Circle, with the participants all around and the performers moving in and out of the circle.

Max bursts into the circle. He has papers everywhere. It's a mess. Max is getting desperate. Government Person joins him with a pile of blankets.

GOVERNMENT PERSON: Hello, Nicoleño. How is the paperwork coming?
MAX: Fine.
GOVERNMENT PERSON: You are able to prove who these tribal members are, correct? We can't just take your word for it.
MAX: Not all of them have proof. But most of them are here. You can interview them directly.
GOVERNMENT PERSON: As your Indian Agent, I will do that, however I need proof on paper that I can send to Washington. Acceptable forms of identification are outlined on page 431.

(Max looks it over. This is bad.)

Best wishes. I need to distribute these blankets as a gift from the government. Here.
MAX: No thanks.
GOVERNMENT PERSON: Then how about some Bibles?
MAX: Whatever.

(Government Person leaves them and goes. Max freaks out as he frantically sorts his impossible pile of papers.
Toni hands out flyers to participants as Antoine crosses.)

TONI: Hey Antoine! Can you give me a hand here?

(Antoine joins Toni.)

ANTOINE: You sure you want my help, I don't identify as gay or transgender or HIV or anything.
TONI: That's OK. You can still be one of us.
ANTOINE: Unless by "us" you mean Native American, because I can't be that. Nothing I can do about it and it may ruin my life.
TONI: Um, if you're looking for pity, you're probably not going to get it from any Indians here. Except maybe your girl Robie.
ANTOINE: We thought it was a secret.
TONI: Not really.
ANTOINE: Well it doesn't matter anymore, we're probably done.
TONI: That's a drag. You know, emotionally, not with heels and a wig.
ANTOINE: It is. You're a member of your tribe right?
TONI: Yup. Grew up on my reservation.
ANTOINE: Do you miss it?
TONI: Every day. But it's not the right place for me anymore.
ANTOINE: Then would it make a difference to you if you weren't enrolled?
TONI: But I'm still Indian?
ANTOINE: You're raised that way but never got the card. Would it change anything?
TONI: Except benefits and stuff, I guess not. Although some days I really want to whip that card out at people. It's exhausting to be

an Indian in L.A. People always ask me, "What are you?" I don't know if they mean a woman or an Indian. It's annoying either way.

ANTOINE: But you could pass as something else right? You don't have to be Indian.

TONI: It's not something you can stop. Even though my people don't accept me, I owe it to them to represent. It's crazy but it's true, I'm always Native above all else.

ANTOINE: I get that.

(Ed joins Antoine and Toni in passing out flyers. Neasha and Bahe join Max.)

NEASHA: Our family tree is a tangled mess, but I think we have it all sorted out here.

MAX: He needs papers. Signed verbal statements. Copies of documents. I can't do it. We'll never get a casino. We won't be rich.

NEASHA: And you'll go to prison.

MAX: That too.

NEASHA: Let me help you. Start with this branch of the tree. We make this Bible look old.

(She crumples the cover and drops it.)

Then we start listing family members as if this was their family Bible.

MAX: But it's not.

NEASHA: I'm saying we beat them at their own game. Keep up, my boy.

MAX: But they'll know.

NEASHA: It's the government, they don't know their right hand from their left. It's our only shot.

MAX: OK. But we have to hurry. You start on Bibles and I'll write up statements.

(They all fill out forms.)

ED: I grew up an Indian without a card. My mom has one but I'm too mixed.

ANTOINE: That's perfect!

ED: Thanks a lot.

ANTOINE: Sorry, I mean for my situation. Did it bother you not to have a card?

ED: Not when I was little. I was raised on my rez and didn't know the difference between enrolled and not enrolled. But I remember the day it changed. I was ten or eleven. My cousins and I went to the park at the end of my street. I played there every day. We were being cool, not messing around or anything, when the tribal police came up. I know these guys. One of them is my neighbor, the other one is my uncle. They know all of us. So they say, "You guys can't be here." I'm like, "Our moms know we're here, José." And he says, "This park is for members of the tribe. If you want to be here you have to have a tribal member with you." Just like that I wasn't an Indian anymore.

ANTOINE: That sucks.

ED: Yeah. I grew up there and it's still my home, but I can't go to half of it without an escort.

TONI: That's messed up.

ED: That enrollment card is nothing and everything.

(Wanda joins Max and company.)

WANDA: Hey, remember me? From when you got arrested?

MAX: Yeah.

WANDA: I heard you're starting a new tribe.

MAX: We are a tribe. We're applying for federal recognition.

WANDA: I've lived all my life in L.A. and I feel Indian. Could I join you guys?

MAX: You're not Nicoleño.

WANDA: But I heard you're letting other people in.

MAX: Well, there may be a couple people that are close to the tribe, tribal members in spirit, that don't technically have papers but do integral work for us. They'll be in.

WANDA: I'm a hard worker. And I respect this land. I recycle and do beach cleanup every year and I even clean the gutters in my neighborhood.

MAX: It takes more than that to be an Indian.
WANDA: I taught myself how to build a sweat lodge and dance pow wow and make my own jewelry and regalia. If I taught myself all that from books and the internet, I can learn your ways.
MAX: I learned my ways from my grandparents.
WANDA: So you're penalizing me because I didn't have grandparents to teach me stuff? Technically what I did is way harder.

(Robie joins them.)

ROBIE: You! I was fine until you showed up and ruined everything.
MAX: Fill out some paper.
ROBIE: What is this?
WANDA: I'll do it.

(Wanda happily goes to work.)

MAX: We're forging documents. Here, make some.
ROBIE: The government is messing with you. There's no way they will accept this in one day.
MAX: They've done crazier things with worse evidence.
EVERYONE: That's right.
WANDA: It is.
ROBIE *(To Wanda)*: What are you doing here?
MAX: Put names in Bibles.

(Max hands the stack of Bibles to Robie.)

Certificates! Xavier has certificates.
WANDA: I know calligraphy.

(Max and Wanda run off together.)

ROBIE: I know everyone loves Max, but this isn't the right way to do this.
NEASHA: I'm sovereign to myself so I have no problem lying to that lying fed.
ROBIE: But why does it have to happen today?
NEASHA: To save your cousin and his art?

ROBIE: Right. But this means . . . What does being Nicoleño mean, really?

NEASHA: To me it means taking care of the land, which includes everything on it. Really connecting to it. Taking care of the ancestors and being a good ancestor in training. Fighting for the ancestors when we have to.

BAHE: All ancestors, not just ours.

NEASHA: Like when they excavated La Plaza downtown. I'd never seen so many human remains in one place. My skin tingled looking out at all those exposed ancestor bones. And all round them shells and arrowheads and bone hairpins. Clearly a graveyard of our people, but they kept digging.

ROBIE: By the time I got there they had kicked everyone out to the street.

NEASHA: So they could cover what they were doing. But we sang and danced all night so the ancestors could hear us and not be afraid.

ROBIE: And that's when the police brought out their riot gear.

BAHE: Those poor people aren't a dancing culture. They fear what they don't understand.

NEASHA: They should have been afraid when they brought the bones out in all those paper bags and threw them into the van, like it was a grocery delivery van instead of a hearse. Can you imagine if we did that to their grandmothers?

BAHE: All those ancestors sitting in storage at UCLA. It hurts my bones to think of them.

ROBIE: We did all we could.

NEASHA: But we failed. Again. I think it's all the failures piled up over the centuries that keep us down today. You can't be beat that many times and not pass it on to the next generations. Today Max reminded me that I've been asleep too long. It's time we rile up and take something back from the people that have taken everything from us. I started this to save him, but I think this recognition can give us a win for once.

ROBIE: If we do this, my kids won't be Nicoleño.

BAHE: Because of Antoine?

ROBIE: It's a secret. But if our kids aren't Indian, who will sing for their bones one day?

NEASHA: If they aren't Indian, no one will dig them up.

NATIVE NATION PROJECT

(Robie, Neasha, and Bahe call to the ancestors. Antoine is bummed out.)

WALTER: What's wrong, Antoine?
ANTOINE: My girlfriend's an Indian and I'm not.
WALTER: Didn't you know that when you started dating?
ANTOINE: Yeah. But I didn't know it would matter so much.
WALTER: Some people are real strict about intermarrying.
ANTOINE: Are you?
WALTER: No. I'm a sucker for love.
ANTOINE: So do you want this application thing to happen?
WALTER: Why not? We deserve to have our tribe recognized again.
ANTOINE: I'm trying to get what it means to be a part of a tribe. I have a family and I've always identified as part of the Black community, but apparently it's not the same thing as a tribe.
WALTER: It's more than the people. There is a place on this Earth that has always been ours. Our DNA is connected to this piece of the planet. We could be anyone, but the land makes us who we are.
ANTOINE: I've heard people say they felt that in Africa. Like everything just clicked for them. I've never felt that.
WALTER: I feel it every time I'm with my tribe on my land. I don't know who I would be without that connection.
ANTOINE: That's deep.
WALTER: It is.

(Max returns with certificates.)

MAX: Just cross out "guilt reduction" and write in "birth."
NEASHA: Make him a birth certificate and get your babies some free government benefits.
ROBIE: We can't just make him an Indian.
NEASHA: Please, the corruption that went on back in the day was rampant. Non-Native people bribed themselves onto the list as Native Americans to get land. That's the point, Robie, this whole government thing isn't our way, it's theirs. Don't let them win another one.

(Robie considers it for a moment, then grabs a certificate and starts writing.)

MAX STORY—SCENE 8

Communal Space

In another part of the circle, Wanda and Max go for certificates.

WANDA: Please, I'm a hard worker. I'll do anything.
MAX: I guess you can help.
WANDA: I just want to belong.
MAX: No promises.
GOVERNMENT PERSON: My scouts tell me there are illegitimate people trying to get into the tribe.
MAX: Not that I know of. Wait, what scouts?
GOVERNMENT PERSON: We need a way to identify who belongs on the reservation and who doesn't. Arm bands? Face paint? Or issue tribal cards?
WANDA: I have a laminator in my car.
MAX: How am I going to make cards and do all of this?
WANDA: I have stickers.

(She pulls out Native American Hello Kitty stickers.)

GOVERNMENT PERSON: This could work in Japan. But use these.

(He pulls out flag and shell stickers.)

MAX: OK. I've got a list of the tribal members here.

(Wanda grabs the list and the stickers and goes.)

WANDA: I'll pass these out.
MAX: But—
GOVERNMENT PERSON: Wait, I heard a rumor about a twinkie or cupcake getting into the tribe. Are you allowing baked goods in? Because that would be a problem.
MAX: No, no twinkies or anything here.
WANDA: Happy to help my tribe cousin.

MAX: OK cousin.

(Wanda puts a shell sticker on proudly. Max keeps quiet.)

GOVERNMENT PERSON: Tick tock.
MAX: I'm nearly done.
GOVERNMENT PERSON: Wonderful. Let's collect everyone and present the papers together. A ceremony.
MAX: Great.

(Government Person goes. Max goes to get certificates.)

ANTOINE/ROBIE STORY—SCENE 5

Communal Space

Antoine and Robie come together. As they talk, Max and Wanda go around giving stickers out. Somewhere in here, Antoine and Robie are given different symbols but don't notice.

ANTOINE: I'm sorry, Robie. I didn't understand how much being a member of the tribe means to you, but I get it now. It's deeper than biology. It's your identity. It's sacred.
ROBIE: We've made you an Indian!
ANTOINE: Wait, what?
ROBIE: We're getting recognition today and we added you to the tribe.
ANTOINE: Isn't there some kind of ceremony or something to do that?
ROBIE: We made you a fake birth certificate.
ANTOINE: You can't do that.
ROBIE: But we did and it's cool. We can get married and have kids. If you still want to.
ANTOINE: I do but . . . I don't want to be a fake Indian. I'm Black. I like that.
ROBIE: But you said you could be Native American.
ANTOINE: If I were to discover that somehow, I would investigate, but there is no way I'm Nicoleño.

ROBIE: Back in the day you became a member of the tribe because the tribe said you were a member. We just did the that for you.
ANTOINE: But those are official government documents. It must be some kind of crime.
ROBIE: We're beating them at their own game.
ANTOINE: I'm not OK with this.

(Xavier takes the stage.)

XAVIER: Hello Urban Rez! It's time for some jokes.
ROBIE: You said you understood why this is so important to me!
ANTOINE: I do. Which is why we have to break up.
ROBIE: Are you serious?
XAVIER: Hey, you two, peace-pipe down. They only gave me one slot on this stage and I've got a lot of material to work on.
ANTOINE: I don't want to be something I'm not to be with you.
ROBIE: I can't give up on my tribe now. We deserve this recognition.
XAVIER: An Indian love poem: You make me feel like a million food stamps.
ANTOINE: You do.
ROBIE: So that's it?
XAVIER: Your breath smells sweet like Shasta.
ANTOINE: I guess.
ROBIE: Can we hug or something?

(They do. It's awkward.)

XAVIER: You are the jelly on my fry bread.
ROBIE: I better see if Max needs anything.
ANTOINE: Yeah. I'll go.
XAVIER: Wait, was that my love poem or my shopping list?

(Robie and Antoine go.)

Young lovers. Boy I've got heaps of good Indian jokes for that, but they'll have to wait for the forty-nine, if you get my meaning.

Try this one out: Three Indians get lost in the forest. Indian One says, "What do we do?" Indian Two replies, "I don't know, we're Indian, we're not supposed to get lost in the forest!" So Indian Three suggests, "Well, when the white man gets lost in the forest, he fires three shots into the air and then somebody comes and saves him." He points to One, "Go ahead and fire three shots." Indian One fires and they wait. After an hour, nothing happens. Finally One asks, "So how long are we supposed to wait?" Two, "I don't know. Maybe we should try again?" Indian One says, "I would, but I only have two arrows left." Aye!!

WANDA STORY—SCENE 5

Communal Space

Wanda matches the list with people, handing out shell or flag stickers.

WANDA: Shell, shell, flag, shell.

(She comes upon Hailey.)

    Hailey, right?
HAILEY: Yeah.
WANDA: Shell for you.
HAILEY: What's this?
WANDA: The sorting.
HAILEY: For what?
WANDA: Who's in and who's out.
HAILEY: Of what?
WANDA: The tribe.
HAILEY: Is this some Urban Rez game because I didn't get orientation for this one.
WANDA: This is not a game, it's the real deal. Max is getting us federally recognized today.
HAILEY: Duh. I know that, but "us" who?
WANDA: The Nicoleños.
HAILEY: I'm already Nicoleño. Who are you?
WANDA: I'm Wanda. Max's letting me in.
HAILEY: He doesn't get to decide.

WANDA: He's doing all the work.
HAILEY: He's not chief.
WANDA: Don't worry about it, you got a shell. You're one of us.
HAILEY: No, I'm one of Max, but I'm not one of you.
WANDA: That's not very cool of you, cousin.
HAILEY: I'm not your cousin.
WANDA: We're all cousins.
HAILEY: That's it. Give me those stickers.

(They struggle. Wanda pulls the list away from Hailey. Wanda rips her shell away and gives Hailey a flag.)

You can't un-shell me.
WANDA: Too late. You've been flagged.
HAILEY: I'm talking to the real tribe.

(Hailey takes off.)

WANDA: You don't know who they are without my list!

EVERYONE

Communal Space

The stage. Max jumps on stage and takes the mic from Xavier. He's a disheveled mess but has a huge stack of papers and Bibles ready.

XAVIER: Hey, I've got two and a half minutes left.
MAX: I need everyone's attention. As you know, I am applying for federal recognition for our tribe. We have a one-time special-session mythical window to apply today. What I need now is to divide everyone into two groups so the tribal members can present the paperwork to the Government Person. Some difficult decisions have had to be made. Everyone with a shell, go to this side. Everyone with a flag go to that side.
WANDA: You heard the man. Move it.

(Everyone in the cast is sorted, some with shells, some with flags. Antoine has a shell, Robie a flag. Families are divided. Government Person joins Max with a string of beads and copper kettles.)

GOVERNMENT PERSON: Wonderful. The great white father has authorized me to give you these gifts as a token of our goodwill.

(Robie notices her sticker is a flag.)

ROBIE: Wait, what? But I'm a tribal member.
MAX: No, you're not. Check the flag.
ROBIE: We're cousins. You came to me today and said I'd be the last of my line. That if I had kids with a non-tribal guy they wouldn't have enough Native blood to be members.
MAX: Well, Antoine's a member and you're not cousins so you can marry into the tribe with him.
ROBIE: But I made him a member. I made that certificate to get him in.
MAX: How could you get someone in if you aren't a member?
ROBIE: Stop it.
HAILEY: This is bogus. That crazy twinkie flagged me.
MAX: She's got the official list, sorry Hailey.
HAILEY: She disenrolled me and you're fine with that?
MAX: I had to delegate. It's tribal government procedure. But once we get recognized you can petition for membership. But you'd better hurry, we're closing enrollment tomorrow.

(Hailey appeals to Neasha.)

HAILEY: Auntie Neasha, you can't be down with this.
NEASHA: It doesn't matter, sweetie.
ROBIE: Auntie, you know who I am.
NEASHA: None of this matters. It's just paper.
ROBIE: But it matters to me.
ANTOINE: Take it.

(He gives his shell to Robie, but Wanda grabs it.)

GOVERNMENT PERSON: You know, if it is your reservation, it really should only have tribal members on it.
MAX: Good point. This is now official tribal business. All you flags gotta go. The rez is closed to you.
WANDA: You heard him. Get out.

(Wanda and Max push people toward the exit.)

ROBIE: No, we're not going!
GOVERNMENT PERSON: I can call in the cavalry to secure the borders.
MAX: What?

(Fighting breaks out. Flags and shells yelling at each other, for each other.)

EVERYONE: I'll give you twenty dollars to get my mom back in. I'm not even Indian. But he's my husband! *(Etc.)*
NEASHA: That's it! This is exactly what the government wants. They want to divide us and pit us against each other until there's no one left.
GOVERNMENT PERSON: Wait, who told you about that?
NEASHA: We don't need a symbol to tell us who we are. I am sovereign!

(Neasha dramatically rips off the flag she got from Hailey.)

WANDA: No! She's the key to the whole family tree.
MAX: Auntie, please. We need you. We need all of you.
NEASHA: You can make something up and apply without me.
MAX: But you won't get the benefits. The billions. The bingo.
ROBIE: What is the point if the tribe isn't all of us?
MAX: The point is . . . the point . . . Wait, what is the point?
GOVERNMENT PERSON: Prison.
MAX: Yes. What about me? And my art?
ROBIE: We won't let you go to prison for art. We'll find an attorney.
MAX: Oh. That's another way to go. But are you seriously going to turn down the billions?
ROBIE: Is it worth billions to lose people you love?

MAX: No. It's not.

XAVIER *(To GP)*: Looks like you lost your game, Fed.

MAX: You said we can choose who stays and who goes, well, we say you go. I am sovereign!

EVERYONE: I am sovereign!

(GP grabs the application from Max.)

GOVERNMENT PERSON: I accept your application. After reviewing it, I officially deny your petition. Ha. I win the day.

ADRIENNE: Who cares? We'll apply again.

HAILEY: Yeah!

GOVERNMENT PERSON: In the past your application was returned for corrections, so you could send it back to us year after year. But once an application has been denied, you may never apply again. A loophole the government built in long ago. Your tribe is extinct forever. Goodbye, Nicoleño, I'll see you in court.

(GP goes.)

HAILEY: Is that true?

ROBIE: We can never be a tribe?

NEASHA: I don't know.

XAVIER: Yes. It's true. Once denied you cannot apply again. I'm sorry.

ADRIENNE: So what are we?

WALTER: Nothing.

TASHA: Welcome to the club.

HAILEY: We're just people? Like Wanda?

(They all look to Wanda. It's bad.)

NEASHA: Oh no.

HELEN: Hey, that's not very nice.

WANDA: No, they're right. I'm no one.

XAVIER: Nobody is no one. *(To Neasha)* For goodness sake, old woman, you've never wanted federal recognition. I don't know what brought each of you here today, but I think most people are

searching for something to heal the disconnect that so many of us feel. You want to be a part of something. To know that you aren't alone. Well like Max and Robie said, we're our own tribe today.
WALTER: It is still our land.
ADRIENNE: And our language.
ROBIE: Nothing's changed. Except . . . I need to tell you guys something. Antoine?
ANTOINE: Yeah.
ROBIE: You stayed and fought for my people, for me. It's not worth it to lose someone you love. If he'll have me back . . . we're dating.
EVERYONE: We know.
WANDA: Really?

(Antoine goes to Robie and they kiss.)

NEASHA: It kills me to admit it, but when you're right, you're right, old man. Like it or not, we are all part of the circle.
XAVIER: That's what Urban Rez is about. Sure, to poke fun at some folks and educate, but it is mostly about reminding us that the circle makes us all stronger.
MAX: It gives all of us a place to belong. Not just me.
ED: I am part of the circle today.
TONI: Me too.
WANDA: Even me?
NEASHA: Yup. Even you. No government can change that. Join me.

(Xavier and others take up hand drums and clapper sticks and sing a song. Neasha takes Wanda's hand to join in a simple social dance.
Others join. Robie and Antoine. Bahe and Tasha. They invite participants to join until every person is part of the dance together.
The song changes to something contemporary and fun. Dance party!
At the end of the dance, participants and leaders enjoy the booths, chat, play games. Eventually Xavier gets back on stage.)

XAVIER: Thanks for joining us at Urban Rez. Don't forget, the marketplace is open up front, so be sure to do some shopping. I've got my eye on a necklace for my sweetie and a granola bar for me. We'll see you out there!

There's a raffle back at the marketplace. Get out there and check your tickets or give them to me.

END

APPENDIX

XAVIER TASKS I

1. Find a member of a California tribe, learn the name of their tribe and one word in their language. .01%
2. Learn the names of three other tribes. .04%
3. Give two examples of the difference between appreciation and appropriation. .38%
4. Collect information from four organizations. .05%
5. Learn the uses of three native plants. .21%
6. Tell one person your ethnic background and learn theirs. .02%
7. Learn an Indigenous social dance. .01%
8. Ask an elder to tell a story from their childhood. .2%
9. Buy something from an Indigenous artist. .03%
10. Tell one joke that makes Xavier laugh (but keep it clean). .05%

Total guilt reduction for all tasks: 1%

APPENDIX

XAVIER TASKS 2

1. Lobby your state to change Columbus Day to Indigenous Peoples' Day. 2%
2. Boycott the Washington Redsk$&ns until they change their name. 4%
3. Go to twelve pow wows and not offend anyone. 7%
4. Every time you want to tell a Native person that they don't look Native to you, don't. 5%
5. When you see a Native image being used in a way that has nothing to do with Native people, call it out. 3%
6. Learn the history of this continent before 1492. 5%
7. Care for the elders, even the ones you don't know. 15%
8. Replant your yard with plants indigenous to your area. 3%
9. Buy ten items from Indigenous artists. 5%
10. Give back the land. All of it. 50%

Total guilt reduction for all tasks: 99%

HOW AN "URBAN REZ" GREW INTO A NATIVE NATION

James E. Garcia

Sometimes you write one play, and sometimes that one play turns into so much more.

Playwright Larissa FastHorse and director Michael John Garcés's *Native Nation* premiered in 2019 at the Salt River Pima-Maricopa Indian Community in Phoenix. The production was a collaboration between Cornerstone Theater Company and Arizona State University Gammage in Tempe. Arizona is home to more than 386,000 Native Americans.

Over the next four years, the trilogy, *Urban Rez, Native Nation*, and its final installment, *Wicoun*, would rise as a collective testament to the universality of the Indigenous experience in North America—and the power of serendipity.

"We didn't intend for it to be a trilogy," said Michael John Garcés.

Indeed *Native Nation*, the trilogy's Arizona installment, wasn't even a glint in the writer's eye until a chance meeting between FastHorse, Garcés, and Michael Reed, senior director of programs and organizational initiatives for Gammage at ASU. They all happened to be on a panel at Western Arts Alliance's conference in Los Angeles in 2016. A presentation about *Urban Rez* piqued Reed's interest so much that he approached them immediately after the discussion to talk about replicating the project in Arizona.

"It was a kind of professional crush from the start," says Reed, who asked them, "Would you guys be interested in talking about doing a show in Arizona, not *Urban Rez*, but something similar in terms of process?"

Initially, Garcés admits, they all thought they "could just adjust *Urban Rez*" for a different state. But FastHorse and Garcés soon realized there were big differences between Native populations in urban Los Angeles versus Arizona.

Arizona is home to twenty-two federally recognized tribes, including the Navajo reservation, the largest in the US, which spans about twenty-five thousand square miles, an area roughly the size of West Virginia.

While each play in the trilogy is told, in Cornerstone fashion, through the eyes of the communities the stories are about, they all have one other thing in common: The plays are not aimed at white audiences.

"My job is to change the face of American theater but also to change audiences," says FastHorse, explaining that when she writes for white theatergoers, her goal is to "get in your head and make you think differently" and "translate the Indigenous experience in a way that white culture will listen and take it in."

Urban Rez, *Native Nation*, and the trilogy's latest iteration, *Wicoun*, are designed to be what FastHorse calls "intentionally incompatible experiences" for non-Indigenous people. While she isn't purposely trying to alienate white theatergoers, the trilogy's narratives avoid any pretense that they need or want a non-Indian stamp of approval. Instead, said FastHorse, these works are created by and for Indigenous people as a way for them to tell their stories the way they want them told.

Based in Los Angeles, Cornerstone has been staging professional theater for more than thirty years "based on the stories, concerns, and issues of a given community." The company uses a mix of professional and nonprofessional artists, the latter cast from the communities where the shows are located. The cast for *Urban Rez*, for instance, included fourteen Indigenous people representing fifteen tribal nations. Cornerstone's method has been perfectly suited for what FastHorse and Garcés wanted the trilogy to achieve.

Vivian Pham, who was a second-year graduate student at UCLA when *Urban Rez* premiered, wrote about the play for *Mapping Indigenous Culture* in 2016.

"*Urban Rez* was an uncomfortable experience from start to finish, because each line documented my and many others' first encounter with the Native American experience," Pham wrote. "Most of us don't know much about the Indigenous people of America. We merely see Native Americans as 'exotics' who own casinos, receive full rides to American universities, and who look like the people featured in Disney's *Pocahontas* . . . never wondering if they've found redemption for all the lives and homeland they've lost."

The characters in *Urban Rez* explore a range of issues: assimilation, water rights, tribal sovereignty, transgender rights, broken treaties, ongoing government duplicity, genocide, and the violation of Indian burial grounds by archeologists who treat ancestral remains like "bags of groceries."

Native Nation raises similar topics, though water rights are addressed with greater urgency, given that some thirty percent of residents on the Navajo reservation do not have running water and the threat of major water shortages looms statewide. (The scarcity of water is one reason for the catastrophic impact of the coronavirus pandemic on Native populations: During the pandemic, The Navajo Nation had the highest rate of COVID-19–related deaths in the country.)

While *Native Nation* is reflective of Indigenous life in Arizona, many of the issues addressed in the trilogy mirror broader concerns in Native country. The topics of environmental degradation, the violation of sacred lands, and the tragedy of missing and murdered Indigenous women in the US and Canada are all addressed in the trilogy.

The works challenge not only persistent stereotypes and misrepresentations of Native people but also what many in Native culture regard as the community's virtual erasure from wider American culture.

"With minimal mention of contemporary issues and ongoing conflicts over land and water rights or tribal sovereignty, Native Americans have become invisible," wrote Crystal Echo Hawk, CEO of the nonprofit IllumiNative, formed to counteract stereotypes and other misconceptions about Native people. "This invisibility," she added, exists across mass media, perpetuating the "omission of contemporary ideas and representations of the ways in which Native people contribute to society."

While most of those cast in *Urban Rez* lived in and around Los Angeles, engaging Indian communities in Arizona took a lot more time and travel. The Hopi and Navajo reservations, for instance, are in northeastern Arizona, the Apache tribes are east of Phoenix, the Havasupai and Hualapai tribes' ancestral lands are in northwestern part of the state, and the Tohono O'odham reservation straddles the US-Mexico border.

FastHorse said directly engaging the communities, as with *Urban Rez*, was critical to the process and spirit of *Native Nation*, adding that nothing made it into the final script without the express approval of the people she wrote about.

"We always went back to our community," said FastHorse, "It's on the land where you discover the moments of collective storytelling, the moments of individual storytelling, the call and response."

FastHorse and Garcés gather narratives and themes that appear in the plays through "talking circles," a traditional practice in which Indigenous people sit in a circle and share stories, concerns, triumphs, and laments.

"I tried not to have any preconceived notions [about *Native Nation*], knowing how Cornerstone works," says Reed, who has worked with ASU Cultural Affairs/ASU Gammage for more than twenty-five years.

Among the most gratifying things about creating the first two plays, said FastHorse and Garcés, has been the change effected in the communities where the plays were created. Cornerstone's work is known to complement or spur activism when it stages a play in a community. The trilogy was no exception. Garcés said the productions helped generate a sense of community and empowerment among the cast, crew, and the shows' largely Indian audiences.

Actor Kenneth Ramos agrees. Raised on the Barona Band of Mission Indians reservation near Lakeside, CA, Ramos is a UCLA graduate with a Bachelor of Arts degree in American Indian studies. He acted in *Urban Rez*, *Native Nation*, and *Wicoun*. Being in the plays changed the course of his life, he says. He's now a full-time actor and member of the Cornerstone ensemble.

The performances gave Ramos room to explore some of the most controversial issues affecting Native people, like "blood quantum," a controversial process developed decades ago by the federal government to determine how much "Indian blood" a person has and whether they qualify for tribal membership.

Describing her experience performing in *Native Nation*, Rosetta Walker, a community activist turned actor, said, "It was beautiful. It was a cast of about forty strangers, forty people from across the [Phoenix] Valley and Arizona, all thrown into a pot to see what kind of cake we could make."

One of Walker's roles involved leading audience members in a discussion about missing and murdered Indigenous women. In real life, Walker was part of a successful grassroots push to pass Arizona House Bill 2570, which established a task force on missing and murdered Indigenous women and girls.

In *Native Nation,* Walker was part educator and part healer. Many in the audience, "didn't know anything about young Native American men and women being abducted, raped, and murdered," she said. Others, namely fellow Native Americans, would say, "This happened to me. I know someone who's missing. My cousin went missing when she was fifteen. Or my auntie was killed in 1976."

Ramos, who grew up knowing little about his Indigenous roots, said, "I'm a product of the kind of empowerment that happens when we see ourselves portrayed in a truthful manner. There's a validation that happens, your perspective is validated. I don't see myself on Netflix. I don't see myself on Hulu. I saw myself in *Native Nation*."

"*How an 'Urban Rez' Grew into a Native Nation*" *was originally published on AmericanTheatre.org on May 21, 2020. Adapted and reprinted by permission of Theatre Communications Group.*

JAMES E. GARCIA is a journalist, playwright, university instructor, and host of the radio show and podcast VanguardiaAmerica.com. He lives with his family in Phoenix.

NATIVE NATION

*Created through collaboration between Larissa FastHorse,
Michael John Garcés, and Indigenous people of Arizona*

PRODUCTION HISTORY

Native Nation was commissioned by Arizona State University Gammage and developed by Cornerstone Theater Company. It was presented by ASU Gammage in association with Cornerstone Theater Company in Akimel O'odham and Tohono O'odham in 2019 at the Salt River Pima-Maricopa Indian Community for two performances on April 20, and at Steele Indian School Park for four performances on April 27–28. The scenic design was by Lynn Jeffries, the costume design was by Meghan E. Healey, the lighting design was by Benajah Cobb, and the sound design was by John Nobori. The production stage manager was Alejandra Maldonado, and the associate director was Michael Garcia. The cast was:

LORETTA TSOSIE	Shyan Bannon
PAULINE	Maria Chavez
LOZEN	Lorraine Cooley
RUSS	Q Crank (Keo)
MR. CLARK	Willis Daychild
CECE	Rae Damon
SHEERAH	Kat Foster
HOUSTON	César Garcia
DENNIS DUNCAN	Peter Howard
SEQUOIA	Dominique Hunter
HENRY	Claude A. Jackson, Jr.
CEHIA	Teya Johnson-Tiger
MODIE	Randy Kemp
CHIEF	Tropix Knight
IRENE	Melissa Leffler

HILLARY	Rocio Marquez
TAMA	Bryce McGertt
BEATRICE	Kennise McGertt
OMARI	Kelcey Mosley
MOLLY	Ceyshe Napa
CATHAN	Kenny Ramos
PHINEAS LONGBOW	Matthew Saraficio
DAMIAN	Adrian D. Thomas
EDWARD	Mario Tsosie
RAESHAWN	Yolanda Tsosie
ANA	Rosetta Walker
VICTORIA	Veronica Williams
TRANSITION CHORUS	Shawn Bitsui, Nora L. Cherry, Iris Chiago, Carol Cooley, Rae Damon, Jade Green, Gloria Halbritter, Taiyne Juan, Arronn Morrato, Rance Sneed and Edith Starr

Community Partners for *Native Nation* included the ASU Center for Indian Education, Native Art Market, Native Health, Phoenix Indian School Visitor Center, the Salt River Pima-Maricopa Indian Community, and Steele Indian School Park.

HOW IT WORKS

Everything is subject to community input and better ideas.

NATIVE NATION EXPERIENCE

The experience is an all-day festival with a marketplace, food, and community performers. During the day, this script is performed twice. The festival experience is before and after the script. No part of the day is raised up as more important than another.

DEFINITIONS OF TERMS

The performance space is a large open circle divided into four directions with a center stage. The audience rotates through the circle during the performance, with a different Activity happening in each of the four directions at a fixed area on the circumference of the circle.

The audience is divided into four groups based on cards they receive when they arrive. In this performance the cards were created by local artists with their information on the back. The words were written in two local languages, so participants had something local and authentic to take home with them. As the group rotates through three of the four directions, their unique Story follows them. (Each group experiences a different Story and participates in three of the Activities in three of the directions.)

Transitions are free-standing pieces of story, music, language, monologues, community performance, dance, art making, etc. They are dramatized as best fits each moment: monologues, in chorus, overlapping, and with movement. They bring the group to the center or spread them throughout the space.

Events are the Ultimate Indian Challenge and include everyone on the center stage of the space. When the Ultimate Indian Challenge Events are happening within the circle, the audience faces toward the center and away from the Activities.

CHARACTERS

Any pronouns or gender-specific references should match the preferred pronoun of the actor. The tribal identification of characters should generally be changed to fit the location of the festival; however, if it is not a location-specific story, the tribal affiliation should match the actor. This script reflects the character names, pronouns, and tribal ID's of the original cast in Arizona.

PHINEAS LONGBOW: Native from Native community/reservation, male

LORETTA TSOSIE: Native raised in non-Indigenous town, female

DENNIS DUNCAN: Non-Native who identifies strongly with being Indigenous, male

HENRY: Elder, Native from a local Native community/reservation, male

BEATRICE: Native from Native community/reservation, Molly's niece, under eighteen, female

MOLLY: Native from Native community/reservation, Beatrice's aunt, female

MODIE: Native from Native community/reservation, male (note: Henry, Beatrice, Molly, and Modie are from the same community)

VICTORIA: Native from Native community/reservation, female

RUSS: Native from the same community as Beatrice, gender fluid

TAMA: Local Native but not enough blood quantum to enroll, same tribe as Victoria, male

RAESHAWN: Native from Native community, female

SEQUOIA: Native from Native community, dating Houston, young adult, female (note: Raeshawn and Sequoia are from the same community)

HOUSTON: Non-Native, dating Sequoia, young adult, male

MR. CLARK: Child Protective Services case worker, male

HILLARY: Native raised in non-Indigenous town, female

SHEERAH: Native from Native community, pow wow–announcer type, female

ANA: Native from Native community/reservation, activist, female

CHIEF: Native from Native community/reservation, Marine veteran, female

EDWARD: Native from Native community/reservation, recent Marine veteran

IRENE: Native from Native community/reservation, recent Army veteran (note: Edward and Irene are from the same community)

CATHAN: Native from Native community, Two-Spirit, twenty-two, male

DAMIAN: Native from Native community, high-school teen, male (note: Cathan and Damian are from the same community)

CEHIA: Native from Native community, pregnant, high-school teen, female

OMARI: Native from Native community, father of Cehia's baby, high-school teen, male

PAULINE: Elder grandma, Native from Native community

LOZEN: Native from Native community, high-school teen, female

CECE: Native from Native community, twenties, female

OPENING

The space is a circle. At each of the four directions is an activity. Between activities are vendors and community tables. A performance stage is in the center.

As participants arrive they are given one of four cards: City, Flower, Eyes, or Rain.

Music plays. It's a festive atmosphere. Perhaps some people play basketball or perform a blessing, as is appropriate to the local tribes and season.

Any signs (restrooms, etc.) are in local Indigenous languages. Elder seating is clearly marked.

There is also a ceremonial space staffed with a counselor or trauma-care worker and different medicines (sage, tobacco, corn pollen, etc.). This space is always open and available.

COMMUNITY STAGE

Local Indigenous folks present anything they like, as long as it is family friendly: story, fashion show, live painting, ceremony, athletic demo, dance, song, music, etc. These pieces should not be curated but supported with an expected time frame and available resources (music, mic, etc.). In the original production, the performances varied in length from just a few minutes to up to an hour, depending on the community.
    The marketplace stays active at this time.
    Sheerah acts as the announcer for each presentation.

SHEERAH: Help me welcome *(Intro of local performer, clothing designer, storyteller, etc.).*

TRANSITION 1

Four people take the stage and recite the names of the recognized tribes of Arizona as a round. This is a way of letting the audience know that that the performance of Native Nation is beginning and calls folks to the circle.

    Ak-Chin Indian Community
    Cocopah Indian Tribe
    Colorado River Indian Tribes
    Fort McDowell Yavapai Nation
    Fort Mojave Indian Tribe
    Gila River Indian Community
    Havasupai Tribe
    Hopi Tribe
    Hualapai Tribe
    Kaibab Band of Paiute Indians
    Navajo Nation
    Pascua Yaqui Tribe
    Pueblo of Zuni
    Quechan Tribe
    Salt River Pima-Maricopa Indian Community

NATIVE NATION PROJECT

    San Carlos Apache Tribe
    San Juan Southern Paiute Tribe
    Tohono O'odham Nation
    Tonto Apache Tribe
    White Mountain Apache Tribe
    Yavapai-Apache Nation
    Yavapai-Prescott Indian Tribe

EVENT ONE

Sheerah takes the center stage.

SHEERAH: Welcome to Native Nation! Hope you've enjoyed our performers. Let's give them a hand! Be sure to keep shopping, but first, let's kick this event off in a good way with Henry and Beatrice.

(Henry and Beatrice join Sheerah.)

HENRY *(In Akimel)*: Creator. Thank you for allowing us to come together at Native Nations to share in our Way (himdag). We ask for blessings to honor our children, our veterans, our elders, and our ancestors. And finally, Creator, help us to guide us back to our blessed water, our blessed food, and our blessed traditions. Guide us, Creator. Amen.

(Henry gestures to Beatrice.)

BEATRICE *(Closing words in Akimel and Diné)*: And we are live tweeting and posting to Instagram at #NativeNationAZ. So follow #NativeNationAZ during and after the show.

(Henry is pleased.)

HENRY *(Using the appropriate greeting for the time of day)*: Now it's your turn to learn some local language. Skeg Tas/Skeg Hwgk niu. Say it back to me. Skeg Tas/Skeg Hwgk niu. Give it a try. Skeg Tas/Skeg Hwgk niu.
GROUP: Skeg Tas/Skeg Hwgk niu.
HENRY: That means "good day/good evening." Here's an easy one: Sapo. All together: Sapo.
GROUP: Sapo.
HENRY: That means "thank you." And finally: Dom nei. Dom nei. Try it with me: Dom nei.
GROUP: Dom nei.
HENRY: That's "see you later." Now you know the proper way to address each other on this land. When you go to any country you learn at least these basic phrases in the local language. All together. Say it to your neighbor. Skeg Tas/Skeg Hwgk niu. Sapo. Dom nei.
GROUP: Skeg Tas/Skeg Hwgk niu. Sapo. Dom nei.
HENRY: Good! Many Native people consider language sacred because it comes from inside a person's soul and is made manifest with the breath of life. Oxygen. The thing we all need to survive. So now we've all shared that sacred thing together. Don't forget it.

(Henry and Beatrice leave as Molly arrives on stage.)

MOLLY: Thank you, Henry, for starting us off in a good way. And thank you to my niece Beatrice. I've always believed that the most important thing we can teach our Native children is to be themselves.

    I am Molly and I am Navajo. I appreciate that a lot of you don't even know why you are here, but you came anyway. Henry helped to remind us that we are standing on Indian land. Native land. And not just because this is a reservation or a special space reserved for Native peoples, but because this entire nation is on Native land. You might even call it a Native Nation, because you never leave our land no matter where you go.

    Answer me this, whose original land are we standing on right now?

(Once she gets some answers . . .)

That's right, we are on Akimel O'odham (and Piipaash) land at this moment. But before that there were other people. And before them, others as well. You should always know whose original land you are standing on, because you are always on Indian land.

(Ana takes over the mic.)

ANA: How often do you non-Natives think of that fact? That your feet are on stolen land? I've heard people say we should get over it. But if your home was taken from you and you still lived there, just in the closet or a shed in the back, you'd be aware of that loss, that anger, every day, wouldn't you? Well that's how it feels to be us, living on our own land and no one seems to care. Most of the time we're invisible to the average American, but not today at Native Nation.

SHEERAH: Thank you. Now, I've prepared a special event just for Native Nation, the first annual Ultimate Indian Challenge!

ANA: Wait, we're going to have fun and continue to appreciate our wonderful Native artists by buying their work. But don't forget, the point of this Native Nation event is activism.

SHEERAH: And to have some laughs.

MOLLY: And protect the water and land.

SHEERAH: And laugh.

MOLLY: And support Native women.

SHEERAH: And laugh!

ANA: Yes, Sheerah, but—

SHEERAH: Ladies, we rehearsed this.

MOLLY: She's right. It's time for the . . .

SHEERAH, MOLLY, AND ANA: Ultimate Indian Challenge!

(Some kind of game show music comes on.)

SHEERAH: I'm your host, Sheerah. And here are your contestants . . .

(Three contestants—Phineas Longbow, Loretta Tsosie, and Dennis Duncan—come forward. Dennis is white-presenting.)

NATIVE NATION PROJECT

Contestant number one, Phineas Longbow, is a member of the Tohono O'odham and San Carlos Apache Nations. He grew up on the reservation and attended TO Community College, Haskell Indian Nations University, and IAIA. That's a lot of Native education.

Contestant number two, Loretta Tsosie, is Diné. She grew up in Phoenix and is working on her master's degree in American Indian Studies at ASU.

Contestant number three, Dennis Duncan, is . . . I'm sorry, I don't have your tribal affiliation here.

DENNIS: I am not currently enrolled in any tribe, but my great-great-great-grandmother was possibly Native American. Unfortunately we cannot prove it, but the story is a treasured one that has been carefully passed down.

SHEERAH: We honor oral history here. What is the story?

DENNIS: That she was possibly Native American.

SHEERAH: Thanks for sharing that.

DENNIS: And my recent DNA test confirmed that I am seven percent Native American. We don't know what tribe but high cheekbones run in our family so we have thought that she was possibly Cherokee.

SHEERAH: Sure. Contestant number three here has a degree in environmental science from the University of Hawaii at Hilo and works to preserve traditional Native American seed banks. That's some important work.

DENNIS: Mahalo.

SHEERAH: This competition will happen in three rounds. We will start with a series of basic history questions. The winner will get the very fancy first annual UIC prize!

(Sheerah unveils some cheesy but impressively excessive prize. The contestants ooh and aah.)

Yes, it's impressive. The first round of the Ultimate Indian Challenge starts now! What year did Columbus get lost and run in to the Americas?

PHINEAS, LORETTA, AND DENNIS: 1492.

SHEERAH: Tie. How many Native American tribes are currently recognized by the American government?
LORETTA: Five hundred and seventy-three.
SHEERAH: Yes, contestant number two gets the point. What is the largest Native American tribe by population?
PHINEAS AND LORETTA: Navajo!
DENNIS: Cherokee!
SHEERAH: Two-way tie for Navajo. Who is the second-largest tribe?
DENNIS: Cherokee!
SHEERAH: Yes. I'm going to hold up two words; point to the one that is usually found at a pow wow.

(The cards say, "avocado toast" and "49." Dennis and Loretta point to "49" with their hands. Phineas points with his lips.)

Trick question, of course the answer is forty-nine, but only contestant number one gets the score for pointing in the Indian way. Same question.

(The first card reads "snag." The contestants laugh.)

Oops. That's the after-hours version. Try this one.

("Tiny Tots" versus "Tater Tots."
 Phineas and Loretta lip point to the "Tiny Tots" first, Dennis hesitates.)

The score goes to contestants number one and two. Although I'd love to have me some Tater Tots at a pow wow. We've got contestants number one and two tied at four each. Contestant number three, you've got some catching up to do with two points. Moving to our Alaska Native cousins, can anyone tell me what the acronym ANCSA stands for?

(Silence.)

LORETTA: Alaska Native . . . something Act.

NATIVE NATION PROJECT

SHEERAH: Time's up. That's the Alaska Native Claims Settlement Act, which was just passed in 1971.

Let's try a physical challenge. Your niece gets sent to ceremony with you at the last minute. When you pick her up, you discover her hair hasn't been done. Let's get three volunteers with hair to come up here.

(Three people are brought up to have their hair done.)

All you have in the car is a dull pencil and two twist-ties, go!

(Our contestants are given pencils and twist-ties and get to work doing hair.)

While they work this out, I've got some jokes for you. Here's an old one. Two white guys and a Native American stand on top of a tall building. The first white guy says, "This is for my people!" and jumps. The second white guys says, "That doesn't make any sense." The Native guy thinks, then says, "Oh, I get it. This is for my people!" and pushes the white guy off.

Why did white men go to the moon? They thought Indians owned land up there too.

Knock-knock! *(Who's there?)*
Emerson. *(Emerson who?)*
Emerson nice moccasins you're wearing.
Knock-knock! *(Who's there?)*
Dewey. *(Dewey who?)*
Dewey have any more fry bread?
Knock-knock! *(Who's there?)*
Arthur. *(Arthur who?)*
Arthur any popovers left?
Knock-knock! *(Who's there?)*
Candy. *(Candy who?)*
Candy knock-knock jokes stop now?
OK, time's up. Let's see what you folks have come up with.

(Phineas and Loretta did OK with different styles. Dennis pulled out their shoelaces to tie a perfect tsiiyééł. Sheerah checks them out and comments on each, then . . .)

The clear winner is contestant number three. The use of your shoelaces is worth double points, so congratulations, you've got yourself back in the game with tied-up scores of four each! Before our next round I've got to leave you with another laugh.

Why hasn't former president Obama returned to attend another rez pow wow?

Too many people asked him to babysit when he was in Standing Rock.

OK, OK. Now down to why we are here: activism!

TRANSITION 2

Cast members move in a circle around the group, calling out the history of water in the area.

Water is life! Water is life! Water is life!

400 A.D.—The Hohokam built canals that populate the Phoenix valley with eighty thousand people.

1880—The Gila River is a mile wide and supports agriculture for the Onk Akimel O'otham and Piipaash peoples. Dams built upriver take eight thousand lives through starvation on the Gila River Indian Community.

1903—On the Salt River, dams alter the Onk Akimel O'odham and Xalychidom Piipaash culture forever on the Salt River Pima-Maricopa Indian Community land.

1981—The Fort McDowell Yavapai Nation stops the building of the dam that would flood half of their nation. They celebrate with the Orme Dam Victory Days.

1988—The Salt River Pima-Maricopa Indian Community Water Rights Settlement Agreement preserves the city of Phoenix by providing water to the city.

2000—The majority of the water for Phoenix comes from Lake Powell, a reservoir along the Navajo reservation. Water levels start to drop dramatically and continue today.

2004—The Gila River Indian Community signs the Arizona Water Settlements Act. A contemporary canal project will bring farming back to the community.

2011—Phoenix is named the "least sustainable city in the world" due to its overuse of water.

2018—The Havasupai people fight to keep uranium mining from contaminating their only source of water. Without that water they will be forced to abandon their homes.

2019—Forty percent of the Navajo people are without running water. The Hopi percentage is higher.

Water is life! Water is life! Water is life!

ACTIVITY ROUND ONE

In Round One, the full activity and story scripts for the first scene of each direction are written out. In following rounds, the activity scripts are not written out, for ease of reading, but where they happen is noted. Activities in each of the four directions are happening concurrently.

Each direction's activity has a script for before and after the Scene 1 story. All activities may not finish to completion. A sound cue lets the actors know when to burst into the activity and start their scene.

Activities are stationary and repeat each round. The scenes rotate clockwise each round so that all participants get to do three activities and complete all of the scenes in their group's story.

ANA: Attention everyone. Listen up! You all got a card when you arrived with the image of a flower, a city, a raindrop, or eyes. That is your group. The point of Native Nation is to get to know new people and learn about new things, so we hope you are in a group with someone other than the people you came with. We split the activities we are doing today into the four directions.

Raindrops, start in the east. City, head north. Eyes, meet in the west. Folks with the flower, go south. That will be your starting activity, and as Native Nation progresses we will rotate you to another direction, so everyone gets to be involved in everything. Go!

(Cast members help divide the attendees into their four directions/groups.)

ACTIVITY NORTH: MISSING AND MURDERED INDIGENOUS WOMEN

Before Scene

The area has a mural backdrop dedicated to MMIW. There are tables with photos of women. A tree sits next to another table with red paper dresses and markers. Other tables hold information.

ANA: I'm Ana. I'm an artist from the Rosebud Sioux Tribe. I put this installation together for two reasons. The subject of Missing and Murdered Indigenous Women is a tough one, but I made this space to focus on action, to educate ourselves and help. It is also a place to celebrate the women's lives, not just the final story as we know it now, but all the good that came before.

Everyone take a card with a story celebrating the life of a missing or murdered Indigenous woman. Then I want you to find a partner and read that woman's story aloud to each other. I want both of you to help each other memorize both women's names. Celebrate their lives. Say their names.

Does anyone need help finding a partner? Raise your hand if you haven't found one yet. Choose who will go first. Then the first person, read the story of the woman whose life is being celebrated. I'll give you about a minute. If you have time after reading it, talk about her life, memorize her name. Then I'll ask the second person to read their card. OK. Go.

(After a minute:)

Now the second person should read their card, if they haven't already. Either way, talk about these women's lives and memorize their names after the stories are read.

NATIVE NATION PROJECT

(After a minute:)

Thank you. Please put the cards back for the next group.

We have many other activities to participate in. Take a red dress and write a note of honor and support for Indigenous women, then tie it to the tree branches.

Learn about the mining and oil extraction industry and the dangers they pose to local Indigenous women. Learn how to get involved.

Appreciate the mural created by Native ASU design students in honor of Missing and Murdered Indigenous Women.

City Card Group Story—Scene 1

While the activity is happening, Irene and Edward spot Chief.

IRENE: Hey Chief!
CHIEF: Hey Irene!
IRENE: Have you met Edward? He's a jarhead like you.
CHIEF: Nice to meet you.
EDWARD: Yeah.
CHIEF: Did you notice? They didn't post colors.
IRENE: The three of us should go to Sheerah and Henry.
CHIEF: But there isn't even a flagpole here.
IRENE: As veterans we should still say something.
EDWARD: I'm good.
CHIEF: But it's unpatriotic.
DENNIS: Excuse me, I've got an AIM flag in my car if that helps.
CHIEF: That's great, but we should have done a full flag ceremony with all the flags.
DENNIS: Like the flags of the tribes.

(Chief pulls out a Marines baseball cap and puts it on.)

CHIEF: And the American flag too.
DENNIS: You have kids in the corps?
CHIEF: No, I am the Marine. Him too. And she's a decorated soldier.

DENNIS: Oh. That must be hard for you.
CHIEF: The Marines aren't known for being easy.
DENNIS: I mean being in the military as Native American people. I've never understood how so many of you serve. That must be such a conflict for you, with the history of the military being used to hunt Native people.
IRENE: Actually the people of this valley have a history of military service that predates the city of Phoenix. And Edward and I are from Gila River—
EDWARD: Leave me out of this.
IRENE: I was just gonna talk about the Ira Hayes parade.
EDWARD: I said leave it alone!

(He storms off.)

DENNIS: Did I say something wrong?
IRENE *(To Chief)*: I should check on him. You good?
CHIEF: I've got this.

(Irene goes.)

Most Native people are proud of their service. Like the families of the Navajo code talkers.
DENNIS: That's different. They were recruited for a special skill, just to speak Navajo.
CHIEF: They just spoke Navajo? They had to learn a code and speak the code in Navajo. That's why they call them "code talkers." They were translating orders from English into code then into Navajo and doing the reverse on the other side while they were being blown up and shot at.
DENNIS: I'm just trying to say that I understand and sympathize with how hard it must have been for you to feel like you had to participate in the American government to get scholarships or whatever.
CHIEF: Isn't it traditionally the warrior's responsibility to protect their land and people?
DENNIS: Yes. But today there are many ways to protect that don't involve the military.

CHIEF: I was called to protect my land and my people through the path of a warrior. My tribe doesn't have a way to do that anymore, so I looked around and saw that the Marine Corps gave me the opportunity to follow my calling to protect my nation. My sovereign nation.

DENNIS: But as a Native American person you certainly can't feel "patriotic" to America.

CHIEF: No, I'm patriotic to my land and my people. Although some Native vets do feel patriotic to America and that's OK.

DENNIS: Then why do you wear the hat?

CHIEF: I'm proud of the service I did to protect my nation and my culture and my people, and I do feel a connection to my fellow Marines in a way that is deeper than I ever imagined it would be, so I wear this cover for them.

DENNIS: But as a Native American person, you have to think about the Long March and the Trail of Tears. I did a paper on the history of the—

CHIEF: You mean the Long Walk? You do a lot of talking to Native people about themselves, but know what, you don't have to believe me or agree with me. That's a value of my tribe that I fought to protect for you. You're welcome.

(Chief goes.)

DENNIS: Thank you!

(Dennis follows after.)

ACTIVITY NORTH:
MISSING AND MURDERED INDIGENOUS WOMEN

After Scene

ANA: Well, while they work things out, let's get back to our activities. I've been involved in Arizona House Bill 2570 for 2019. It passed the House and the Senate committees, but we need you to urge your senator to get it on the calendar for final passage.

Here are some Native American women from history that you may or may not have heard about in school:

- In 1902, Eliza Burton Conley, from the Wyandot tribe, was the first woman admitted to the Kansas Bar.
- In 1985, Wilma Mankiller was the first female chief of the modern Cherokee tribe and awarded the Presidential Medal of Freedom. However, the first Native American to receive the Medal of Freedom was the Legendary Mother of the Navajo Nation, Annie Dodge Wauneka, in 1963.
- Elizabeth Peratrovich, Tlingit, petitioned Alaska Governor to introduce the Anti-Discrimination Act of 1945. The first of its kind in an American territory or state, the groundbreaking law prohibited racial discrimination in public accommodations and facilities. Her powerful testimony is still celebrated annually.

Thank you for participating. Please be sure you read more, and leave a dress on the branches.

ACTIVITY EAST: WATER

Before Scene

Hillary has many buckets of water on one side of her and tables of information on the other, about watersheds and local water issues/actions and how people can get involved.

HILLARY: The Indigenous people of this land have always been on the frontlines of water issues, but we need all of you to help. My husband and I were at Sacred Stone Camp for a month as water protectors. Mni Wiconi! We've always considered ourselves committed to the cause, but when we got the first ruling in our favor from the Supreme Court to stop the pipeline . . . I was hit so hard. Celebration was happening all around us, but I just wanted to cry, because I realized in that moment that after five hundred years of losing, I had believed in my heart that we would lose.

But when I saw the young people celebrating I realized that for the first time in a century, we have a generation who knows what it feels like to win. That knowledge, that hope, that is the most powerful weapon our Nation has to change the future for us all. Now it's our turn to make a choice to help protect the water and Mother Earth.

To help us think about water in our own lives, I'm going to read a series of statements. If you agree with the statement, if it applies to you personally—I invite you to raise your hand. Let's try one for practice: I am right-handed. If you agree with that statement—if it's true for you—raise your hand. Well done, righties. I think we're ready. Here we go.

- I know where my water comes from.
- I think about water conservation.
- I actively work to conserve water.
- I have always had access to clean, safe drinking water.
- I have lived in a home without running water.
- I have had to carry my own water.
- I am worried about the future of water in this region.

Speaking of carrying water: These twenty five-gallon buckets hold one hundred gallons of water and represent the amount of water the average American uses in ONE DAY. According to the UN, a minimum recommended daily amount is fifteen gallons per person per day. However, one of our Native Nation family grew up on the Salt River Pima-Maricopa Indian Community without running water and her family survived on less than one gallon of water per person per day.

We also have information on the table about other threats to the water. Standing Rock is best known, but the fight continues in many places including right here in Arizona.

"You don't know the value of water until you have to carry it." Let's carry our own water from one side of this area to the other and realize that many people today still carry their water long distances.

Rain Card Group Story—Scene 1

Molly addresses the group, which includes Mr. Clark.

MOLLY: People don't realize that saving the water and the Earth isn't a choice. Saving those things saves us. Walking three days to Oak Flat was one of the most intense experiences of our lives, right?

BEATRICE: I've never been so tired.

MOLLY: We walked through a terrible storm and even saw lightning strike a bush and start it on fire.

MR. CLARK: That sounds dangerous.

MOLLY: It was at times, but we were walking to protect a sacred site.

MR. CLARK: And your niece was with you?

MOLLY: Absolutely. We do everything together.

MR. CLARK: Including spending six months, much of it in winter weather, at Standing Rock?

MOLLY: Do I know you . . .

BEATRICE: Yeah. Did you see my aunt on the news? She was on CNN.

MOLLY: Well, we are here to support Native Nation today. There are current issues right here in Arizona.

MR. CLARK: My name is Mr. Clark. I work for Child Protective Services and I am here to investigate the welfare of this child.

MOLLY: My brother has not been in contact with us for—

MR. CLARK: I'm not investigating Beatrice's father, I am investigating you.

MOLLY: Why?

MR. CLARK: Because Beatrice barely got passing grades last year and is on the edge of being held back for missing too much school this year. Education is important.

MOLLY: She is getting educated in geography, Earth sciences, physical fitness, and learning the ways of many Native Nations, including our own.

MR. CLARK: The state requires a formal education and you, as the foster guardian of Beatrice, are responsible for making sure Beatrice goes to school, not on camping trips.

BEATRICE: It's my fault. I don't study enough. She tells me to. I'll do better.

MR. CLARK: I'm glad to hear that, but it is your guardian's responsibility. I tried to talk about this in private, but you ignored all of my requests for a meeting.

MOLLY: Our phone is out of minutes.

MR. CLARK: I sent emails.

MOLLY: We have to go to town for internet.

MR. CLARK: I sent letters.

MOLLY: We have been . . .

MR. CLARK: At another protest?

MOLLY: We are not protesters, we are protectors.

BEATRICE: I can do homeschool. Catch up.

MR. CLARK: Perhaps, but in light of your aunt's lack of response, I have the authority to remove you to a more stable situation while the investigation—

MOLLY: No!

MR. CLARK: We always try to place the children with family members first. Is there someone else?

MOLLY: If there was, I would not be raising Beatrice alone.

MR. CLARK: Then I will be removing Beatrice while I investigate.

BEATRICE: No. Please. Let me stay!

MR. CLARK: I'm sorry, but this is the best thing.

BEATRICE: I won't go!

MR. CLARK: There is a nice group home for tonight.

BEATRICE: I'm not going to some foster-kid shelter.

(Beatrice turns. Molly reaches out and grabs Beatrice's arm.)

Let go of me!

MOLLY: I won't let them take you away from me.

MR. CLARK: That's for CPS to decide.

MOLLY *(To Beatrice)*: Please, don't make this worse.

BEATRICE: You're hurting me!

MR. CLARK: That is unlawful restraint of a minor.

(Scared, Molly lets go. Beatrice runs.)

MOLLY: I'll get her.

MR. CLARK: No, I will. You stay here.

(Mr. Clark goes, leaving Molly unsure what to do. Victoria arrives.)

VICTORIA: What was that?

MOLLY: The state is going to take Beatrice away from me.

VICTORIA: They can't do that.

MOLLY: They are. It took me a year of fighting to get Beatrice in my home the first time, if I go against the CPS case manager now I'll never get her back.

VICTORIA *(Looking around)*: Let's talk about this somewhere else.

MOLLY: No. I want witnesses. *(Loudly)* My brother is incarcerated. He made mistakes, but incarceration rates for Native people have jumped ninety percent in the past twenty years. Don't tell me the system was fair for him. The state says they always place the child with a family member when possible, but that's not true for Native children. Our children are taken from us first, then we fight to get them back.

VICTORIA: We'll call the Indian Child Welfare Act representative.

MOLLY: Our ICWA rep sided with the state last time. Against me.

VICTORIA: But they exist to keep our children in Native homes.

MOLLY: I had to fight alone last time. I'll do it again.

VICTORIA: You aren't alone now.

MOLLY: First we need to find Beatrice before CPS does. I'll check the parking lot.

(Molly goes.)

VICTORIA: I'll spread the word.

(Victoria goes.)

ACTIVITY EAST: WATER

After Scene

HILLARY: OK, sorry about that. Let's focus back on why we are here and get specific to Arizona. On average, each Arizona resident uses about one hundred and forty-five gallons per day. That's worse than the national average, and in the desert.

The Colorado River system, which supplies thirty-six percent of Arizona's total water use, has experienced extensive drought conditions for the past nineteen years. This has resulted in Lake Mead dropping to historically low reservoir levels. Most recent projections show a probability of shortage soon.

But there are things we can do to conserve:

- When washing dishes by hand, don't let the water run. Fill one basin with wash water and the other with rinse water.
- If you drop an ice cube, don't toss it in the sink, throw it into a plant.
- Garbage disposals use gallons of water; compost fruits and vegetables instead.
- From the laundry room, have a plumber reroute your graywater to trees and plants instead of the sewer line. But check your city's codes first.
- If you shorten your shower by one minute, you can save one hundred and fifty gallons of water a month.
- Turn off the water while you lather your hair and save another one hundred and fifty gallons a month.
- In your yard, always choose our beautiful indigenous plants that thrive on the desert climate.
- Always use a pool cover. It keeps it clean, reduces chemicals, and prevents evaporation.
- Technology has come a long way. Check that all of your water-using products have WaterSense labels to conserve.

There are so many more ways to conserve our water supply for the future. For more ideas go to wateruseitwisely.com.

ACTIVITY SOUTH: APPRECIATION OR APPROPRIATION

Before Scene

Appreciation or appropriation? Raeshawn leads a space with information about Not Your Mascot, Beyond Buckskin, etc. There is a little stage for the skit, very cheesy and fun.

RAESHAWN: Is this appreciation or appropriation? You decide.

(Russ and Cehia come out in Redskins shirts. They play out a skit with Modie and Damian.)

MODIE: Your shirt is a racial slur as defined by the dictionary!
DAMIAN: Love the team, hate the mascot!
CEHIA: Go Skins!!
MODIE AND DAMIAN: Boo! Racist!
RAESHAWN: What do you think?

(After people respond:)

CEHIA: Forget it. I came to enjoy the game.

(Cehia goes. Russ stops.)

RUSS: Look, I appreciate what you're saying, but I'm here. What do you want me to do?
MODIE: Turn the shirt inside out.
RUSS: Seriously?
DAMIAN: Yes. Show your team's colors, not their racism.
RUSS: OK.

(Russ takes the shirt off and puts it back on inside out.)

MODIE AND DAMIAN: Yea! Thank you! Appreciate your team, not the mascot!

(Russ goes.)

RAESHAWN: How about this one, appreciation or appropriation?

(Russ and Cehia come out in bad Native Halloween costumes.)

That's an easy one right? But look at what happens next.

(Modie and Damian pull out protest signs against Yandy, the costume maker.)

DAMIAN: We just want to talk. You say you want to honor us with your products, then why won't you speak to us?
RUSS: The police have been called!
MODIE: For what? Wanting to talk?
RUSS: The police are on their way now.
RAESHAWN: We are a culture, not a costume. But what if the piece looks authentically Native? Is that appreciation or appropriation?

(Cehia puts on a beaded necklace. Russ puts on a Native-made piece of jewelry.)

Cehia, do you know where your necklace came from?
CEHIA: Etsy?
RAESHAWN: But was it made by a Native American artist?
CEHIA: I don't know. They had free shipping.
RAESHAWN: So it could be appropriation but you don't know. It could have been made anywhere by anyone. Why not buy authentic pieces instead? Russ, where did your jewelry come from?
RUSS: A member of the [tribe]. *(Russ ad-libs something about the provenance of specific piece(s) of jewelry they are wearing)*
RAESHAWN: If you always buy Native-made products from Native people, you can wear them proudly. And that's appreciation.

(The performers take a bow.)

To help us think about these issues in our own lives, I'm going to ask you to get into groups of two or three. Find someone.

Each person in the group should share an example of when you have appreciated something from another culture. Tell them why it is appreciation, not appropriation. Really make sure it is a real example from your experience.

(After a couple minutes) Now each person in the group should share an example of appropriation that they have experienced or witnessed, and what they found challenging or problematic about it.

Each person in the group should tell a story about an example of positive change with regard to appropriation—a time when appropriation was ended or turned into appreciation in an appropriate way.

There are other activities to explore. We have more examples of appreciation versus appropriation on both sides of the booth.

If you shopped from one of our Native marketplace vendors, be sure to take a selfie and hashtag us at #NativeNationCTC and #NativeNationAZ.

Or post a story telling about your experience of appreciation.

Flower Card Group Story—Scene 1

Houston comes up and greets Sequoia affectionately. Sequoia pulls away nervously.

HOUSTON: Sequoia, please don't do that.
SEQUOIA: What?
HOUSTON: Flinch when I'm close to you. It's hard not to take it personally.
SEQUOIA: It's not personal and you know it.
HOUSTON *(To group)*: We have been dating for a year and still have to keep it a secret from her family. That's weird right?
SEQUOIA: Shhhh!
HOUSTON: There's no one from your family here.
SEQUOIA: But there are Indians here. *(To group)* We officially get all offended if someone asks if we know the one Native American person they know, but the truth is . . . we probably do. Or at least know someone who knows them. We're like two percent of the American population. How can we not know each other?
HOUSTON: Well it's too late now. So if one of you knows Sequoia's family, please don't tell them that we've been dating for a year, because my showing up at every family gathering for the past seven months hasn't been obvious.
SEQUOIA: I told them we're just friends.
HOUSTON: But why? They like me. *(To group)* I'm likable, right? I don't come across as a serial killer? I mean you've only known me a few seconds but it's gone OK, right?
SEQUOIA: I am trying to protect him. My family is large and in everyone's business. I mean IN it.
HOUSTON: I'm already in it with them. I can take it.

SEQUOIA: You can take being my friend; when you're my boyfriend it will all change. Suddenly you're the enemy. Trust me, they've run off nearly every boyfriend I've had.

HOUSTON: Wait, *nearly* every boyfriend? You never said "nearly" before.

SEQUOIA: Oh, there were a couple they liked. But I didn't. That's all that matters.

HOUSTON: Who did they like?

SEQUOIA: Well I am pretty sure one of them was a distant cousin. Which inappropriately made my family happy, but not me.

HOUSTON: Who else?

SEQUOIA: Just a guy from high school.

HOUSTON: A Native guy, right?

SEQUOIA: Since I went to a Native high school, yes.

HOUSTON: So the two guys they have been OK with were Native?

SEQUOIA: Stop it. We aren't talking about this now. Here.

HOUSTON: Why not? We're here to talk about Native issues.

SEQUOIA: This isn't an issue.

HOUSTON: Your family isn't OK with you dating non-Native guys. That's an issue for me.

SEQUOIA: Not a Native-specific one. Lots of people like to date in their culture.

HOUSTON: Yes, scary people who do marches for Confederate statues.

SEQUOIA: Are you comparing my people to white supremacists?

HOUSTON: I'm just saying that it's a thing that no one talks about but it's there and I think that's the real reason you won't tell your family about us. If "Native Nation" isn't the place to talk about this, where is?

SEQUOIA: OK, do my people feel more comfortable with people from my culture? Of course they do. There's only a few of us on the planet that share the same history. That doesn't make them prejudiced.

HOUSTON: I think it does.

SEQUOIA: You can't possibly understand what it feels like to have the federal government try to make your people extinct. And they are still doing it, trying to destroy us.

HOUSTON: That's horrible. And I don't know what that feels like, but I do understand being different and alone. And I have really worked hard to learn about your people. I think I've earned a little respect.

SEQUOIA: I love you, but there is nothing you can do that will make you one of us. That's just a fact.

HOUSTON: I'm not trying to be one of you. I'm trying to be with you.

SEQUOIA: It's really complicated.

HOUSTON: So explain it.

SEQUOIA: Not here.

HOUSTON: Why not? We are here to educate folks. Educate us right now. I get it, I'm not one of you. But I have the right to take the heat with your family. Unless you are the one that has a problem with my race?

SEQUOIA: It's not just me.

HOUSTON: It is you?

SEQUOIA: No, I mean . . . it's bigger than all of us.

HOUSTON: That doesn't make sense.

SEQUOIA: It's a complicated time for my tribe. We just got the new casino and everything is changing. The tribal police are getting super strict about non-members on our land. We need to wait until things calm down.

HOUSTON: But how long will that be?

SEQUOIA: Soon. Indian time . . . Hopefully this year.

HOUSTON: Hopefully? So it could be next year?

SEQUOIA: I don't know. Let's just see.

HOUSTON: So we can't get married or have kids until next year?

SEQUOIA: Whoa. Get married? Kids? We haven't talked about any of that.

HOUSTON: I kind of assumed that is where we were heading. Didn't you?

SEQUOIA: Ummm . . . I guess so.

HOUSTON: So we're both thinking of that.

SEQUOIA: Yeah.

(They kiss.)

HOUSTON: So we're going to tell your family today?

SEQUOIA: No.

NATIVE NATION PROJECT

(She goes.)

HOUSTON: Wait!

ACTIVITY SOUTH: APPRECIATION OR APPROPRIATION

After Scene

RAESHAWN: Sorry for that interruption. But did you know that appreciation and appropriation of Native American contributions goes beyond fashion?

- Two of the earliest founders of the US women's movement, Elizabeth Cady Stanton and Matilda Joslyn Gage, were guided in their ideals by Haudenosaunee women.
- The Haudenosaunee were also the model for the three branch, representative democracy of the United States of America.
- The participation of Native Americans in the military is higher than any other ethnic group.
- Native American Sign Language had a strong influence on the development of American Sign Language.
- Native Americans in New England introduced the settlers to chewing gum made from the spruce tree.
- Both field hockey and ice hockey are based on a game called shinny. This Indigenous stickball game was played throughout North America well before the European arrival.

Is there a way you can better appreciate the contributions of Native American people to your life? Think about it.

Please keep taking and posting those selfies and don't forget to tag us at #NativeNationCTC and #NativeNationAZ.

ACTIVITY WEST: FOOD

Before Scene

The area has several tables with prepared food, drink, and information about indigenous foods.

TAMA: I'm Tama from Salt River Pima-Maricopa Indian Community where I grew up with my mom and her people. When I was young I used to hear the elders talk about hunting and fishing and gathering that they don't do anymore and I thought to myself, this is sad, but things change. We have Wally World and Bashas. You know, we have stores now so we're fine. Even though I grew up eating in stores, something inside knew that when the apocalypse came, we would survive. We could go back to the old ways and get our own traditional food, no problem.

I started looking into the indigenous plants that we used to eat and discovered that they aren't just scarce, they are gone. Pesticides and insecticides have leaked from non-indigenous lawns and decimated the natural plants.

Last year my aunt and I counted every food plant we could find in a couple day's radius of our home on the rez. If we harvested everything, like we're completely irresponsible and left nothing behind, we wouldn't have nearly enough food to last the year. In fact we'd be dead in months. Food sovereignty isn't an abstract concept about organic eating or big farming, it is life and death for us.

But we are fighting back by growing traditional foods and relearning what our bodies need. I have dedicated my life to changing that and here you will help me.

Our Hopi chef, Derick Melvin, and our Yaqui tribal member Esther Almazan have prepared special treats for us: a prickly pear cactus juice from Tuscon, and an indigenous food that his grandma called "blue marbles."

(As the offerings are passed out) The pövölpiki or blue marbles are made with three ingredients: blue corn flour, culinary ash, and water. Hopi corn contains thirty percent more protein than other varieties. The culinary ash adds essential minerals—sodium, potassium, calcium, magnesium, manganese, iron, copper, and zinc.

Take a moment to appreciate the beauty of the food and drink you are tasting. The colors and textures have meaning. They feed both the body and the spirit. They are sustainable in this climate. Think about the generations of people before us who have used these ingredients and the generations to come. This food and drink make us a part of a line of humanity stretching through all of time.

Thanks for sharing that together. We have other information here including cookbooks with Native American recipes, the story of the Hopi corn, and information about our locally sourced prickly pear cactus juice.

To help us think about food in our own lives, I am going to label the four corners of this square ALWAYS, SOMETIMES, RARELY, and NEVER. I'm going to make a statement, and I'm going to ask you to move to the corner that most applies to you. Again, the corners are ALWAYS, SOMETIMES, RARELY, and NEVER. When you get to your corner I'll give you further instructions. Here we go.

I know what fruits and vegetables are in season.

In my home we use foods that are indigenous to the area.

OK, great. I hope each of you has found your corner. Now I'd like folks in each group to introduce themselves to each other and then find one thing that you all can agree on around food and why you chose that corner. Pick one volunteer in each group to share back to the rest of us. I will give you a moment to find something in common then we will share them with the group.

(After a couple minutes) Great, let's find out what you have in common. If you have not yet found something in common, just share a bit about what came up in your conversation.

Eyes Card Group Story—Scene 1

Cathan and Omari do their food activity.

CATHAN: I appreciate all of this but it's too late. The apocalypse is already here. Back home people are dying every day from bad food and curable diseases and alcohol and drugs and rejection. I'm twenty-two years old and I've already been to so many funerals, I can't even count them all. I hear my phone buzz and I don't think, "Who's texting me?" The first thing I think is, "Who died?" I don't want to feel like that anymore.

OMARI: I looked around at my family: one side is Native on the rez and the other side is African American here in the city, and I realized that I have all these great-aunts and uncles and all of my grandparents on the Black side, but on the Native side, they're already gone.
CATHAN: That's not OK.
OMARI: Yeah, but that's why we're doing this Native Nation thing. To educate people and stuff.
CATHAN: So you and I eat better and whatever. What about all the people back home who couldn't come? The ones that really need help?
OMARI: We bring some seeds back and plant a garden.
CATHAN: It's not enough.
OMARI: It's a start.

(Lozen joins them. She looks really concerned.)

LOZEN: Cathan! Did you see Facebook?
CATHAN: Don't tell me. I can see by your face that I don't want to know.
OMARI: What?
CATHAN: I'm serious.

(Cathan starts to go.)

LOZEN: Everyone will be talking about it at Grandma Pauline's tonight.
CATHAN: Fine. What?
LOZEN: It's Luanne.
CATHAN: She's dead.
LOZEN: No, but she tried.
CATHAN: Because of the coming-out ceremony?
LOZEN: I think it was a lot of things. But she was really upset after Samantha's ceremony.
CATHAN *(To Omari)*: This is what I'm talking about. How is a garden going to keep Luanne alive?
OMARI: Luanne's thing is more complicated. Being trans is hard everywhere.
CATHAN: But our own people are making it worse.

OMARI: What happened at the ceremony?

LOZEN: They wouldn't let her dance with us girls.

OMARI: Ceremony is really strict. Men do men's parts and women do women's parts.

LOZEN: Grandma helped her make a new i:pud and everything. She was so excited.

OMARI: Luanne had to know those old traditional guys wouldn't let her switch.

CATHAN: No, she didn't know because traditionally our people saw Two-Spirit and gender-fluid people as special.

LOZEN: Grandma Pauline taught us all about Hosteen Klah. He's not from TO, but he used his special medicine to help and protect people.

OMARI: Hosteen wasn't trans.

LOZEN: But Hosteen used Two-Spirit medicine.

CATHAN: Exactly. He reminded us that people like me and Luanne have important medicine that can bring the people together.

OMARI *(To Cathan)*: Look, with you it's different. People back home are cool with the gay thing.

CATHAN: Are you kidding me?

OMARI: Not everyone, but people love you. You were prom king and queen.

CATHAN: Omari, most people voted for me as a joke.

OMARI: But you went and won them over. It was the best prom we've ever had.

LOZEN: People still talk about it at school.

CATHAN: What about Luanne?

OMARI: But being trans and expecting to change traditions like who does what at ceremony? That's totally different.

CATHAN: But I just said that it is traditional—

OMARI: Everyone says that, but what were the specifics? It was a long time ago that people believed that way. But we do know how this ceremony works, and we are super specific about the details because that's how it's been passed down to us and how it's going to be passed down for the future.

CATHAN: But things change. Men didn't wear jeans back in the day but they do now, even when they dance.

LOZEN: Ribbons and cotton dresses are new too.

OMARI: I'm on your side. I'm on Luanne's side. I just think she could have picked her battles better.

LOZEN: Are you blaming the victim? Remember Alexia? She was attacked in daylight walking home not just for being trans, but for defending a gay kid. She picked that battle because it was the right one.

OMARI: Of course it was.

LOZEN: After that she moved to the city and never came back.

OMARI: At least she found a way out that wasn't suicide.

CATHAN: But that shouldn't be the only way out. We shouldn't have to choose between our people and being who we are and feeling safe. And it doesn't just affect us. Alexia's grandmother asks about her all the time. Her cousins miss her. She lost her people and her people lost her.

LOZEN: Luanne stayed and tried to do everything right, and that still wasn't enough for people.

OMARI: You know I hate that she felt like suicide was her only choice. No one should feel like that. Ever.

CATHAN: That little kid who did it last year was only eleven.

LOZEN: It's getting worse, not better.

OMARI: I know. If people are going to stay on the rez, they need help. That's why we're here today. To bring back new ideas. To feel connected to something bigger.

CATHAN: But our culture should be enough.

OMARI: Our culture has been changed by colonization. Everything has. We weren't so isolated before. There were way more of us and other Native people all around.

LOZEN: So we're stuck? Stay isolated or leave?

CATHAN: I can't go to another funeral. We have to do something more, Lozen. And we have to do it now.

LOZEN: What can I do?

CATHAN: Get all our cousins and friends who are here at Native Nation together for a meeting. I'm going to get us some help.

OMARI: What kind of help?

CATHAN: The best kind. I'm going to find Grandma.

(They all go.)

NATIVE NATION PROJECT

ACTIVITY WEST: FOOD

After Scene

> TAMA: OK, sorry about that, but to get back to why we're here at Native Nation, let me tell you a bit more about our foods. Native foods are having a huge impact nowadays—Native American food is the original "farm to table" and no foods are more local than indigenous ones. Here are some facts about the impact that Native American agriculture has had on today's society:
>
> - Today, sixty percent of the world's food supply comes from American Indian agricultural methods.
> - All major varieties of corn (red, blue, white, yellow) that are available today were already available to the Native Americans when the Europeans first arrived in the New World. Those foods are now a staple worldwide.
> - These are just some of the other foods that are originally from the Americas—some may surprise you: potatoes, tomatoes, bell peppers, chili peppers, avocado, blueberries, cranberries, strawberries, quinoa, cashews, pecans, peanuts, and vanilla.
> - Some dishes that originated with the original peoples of this land that are still eaten today: pancakes with maple syrup, cornbread, tortillas, grits, fried green tomatoes and succotash.
>
> Keep exploring and find new ways to use our beautiful indigenous foods.

TRANSITION 3

Two women of different generations take the center stage, drawing the participants out of their activities and back into one group. They alternate monologues from the stage.

> In 1930 my grandmother ran away to Phoenix Indian School and the first thing they did was cut off her hair.
>
> *In 2018 my son's school sent a letter that said we had to prove that his braids were culturally significant or cut them off.*
>
> I have a picture of my grandma's class. I see those children in identical uniforms and short hair and feel sad for all they lost.
>
> *My son got a lot of bullying at school. The kids stopped him from going to the boy's restroom and said he had to use the girl's.*
>
> But I also know that my grandmother came from a family of migrant farm workers. She ran away to Phoenix Indian School because she loved the structure. She had a roof over her head and her first real bed. She had friends and got to learn every day.

There were hard times there, but she always said that it was better than what she came from.

At ten, my son had enough and asked us to cut off his hair. It killed me. I asked his teacher if we could make a presentation to his classmates. I explained to them that his long hair isn't just a style, it's a tradition that means a lot. My son played flute for his class. After that the other kids had some respect for him. But then I got that letter from the school.

My grandmother stuck with her education and became a teacher. She championed the underdogs, inner-city youth, and "trouble" children. She was an amazing woman. I do what I do now because I want to help kids like she did.

Governor Lewis heard about the school telling my son to cut his hair. He has long hair too and told my son to be proud of his hair. He got us the letter, but I can't believe that a school today, built on the homelands of our own people, the people who built these canals, is still so ignorant.

(Together) Hair is more than fashion to us. It's culture. Family. Resistance.

EVENT TWO

SHEERAH: Hope your first round of activities went well. Before we move to the next one, it's time for more of the Ultimate Indian Challenge! For this round we are going to play a traditional Indian game. Shoot, it's probably the most traditional pan-Indian game there is, played from Alaska to Arizona.

DENNIS: Lacrosse?

(Sheerah tosses a basketball to the contestants.)

SHEERAH: No, basketball! No matter where you are in Indian country, never schedule something against a basketball game. No one will show up. So, we've got a special Ultimate Indian Shoot-out for you.

(Some kind of game that includes trivia questions to get an occasional advantage. It's meant to be silly and fun, not super serious. These trivia questions are samples that can change in content and number as needed.)

How many federally recognized tribes are in Arizona? (22)
What year did the Roosevelt Dam open? (1911)

On what Indian land do the Rockies and D-Backs play during spring training? (Salt River Pima-Maricopa Indian Community)

Speaking of Salt River, what does the "Man in the Maze" represent? (The journey a person makes through life, includes hardships and obstacles)

Now a few casino questions:

The Hon-Dah Resort Casino is operated by what tribe? (White Mountain Apache)

Which tribal casino has the cheapest cost for crab legs at $28.95? (Fort McDowell Casino)

Which Arizona tribe has the highest per cap?

(Silence.)

Ayee, just kidding.

"Hey Victor!" is a popular quote from what Native American hit movie? (*Smoke Signals*)

Second round gets tougher. Each shot is worth three points. Let's talk about another Indian favorite, fry bread. OK, quick PSA, fry bread is full of fat and empty carbs and should only be consumed in moderation. That said, we know we all love it. Here's a series of questions about fry bread. What is the difference between most fry breads and bannock?

PHINEAS: Milk.

SHEERAH: Yes. One point.

PHINEAS: I thought the second round was three points.

SHEERAH: Right. Triple it.

What state made fry bread their official bread in 2005?

DENNIS: South Dakota.

SHEERAH: Correct. What is a South American dish that is nearly identical to fry bread?

LORETTA: Cachanga! Thank you second semester abroad.

SHEERAH: That's right. Three points each.

The Apache say that when someone makes their first piece of fry bread it brings this . . . ?

PHINEAS: Snow.

SHEERAH: Very good. And that's our second round of competition. Let's give these competitors a hand.

TRANSITION 4

Cast members call out from the edges of the space, opening the group away from the center. Excitement builds for the different foods.

    Fry bread hamburgers
    Blue cornmeal
    Tepary beans
    Piccadilly
    Steam corn
    Cemit
    Mutton stew
    Spam
    Cholla buds
    Posolc
    Nopales
    Acorn stew
    Indian tacos
    Mexican food!

    (Everything stops. What?!?)

Come on, even though Indians get swept up in the immigration raids on Mexican restaurants and end up in District Eight, we still can't resist that Mexican food. Am I right?

ACTIVITY ROUND TWO

HENRY: Native Nation, I need your attention for an announcement. We have a missing girl, Beatrice. You all saw her at the beginning with me. Fourteen, long hair, glasses, eagle on her shirt. If you see her, please report it to one of the activity stations in the four directions.

Speaking of activity stations, it's time to rotate to your next activity. Remember the card you got at the beginning; it's time to join that group in a new direction. If you have the city card, go east. The card with the eyes should head north. Flowers to the west, and the raindrops go south. Get moving to join your new activity.

(Activities begin, then Scene 2 of all stories interrupts the activity.
The activity scripts will not be repeated but each activity is noted at the top of the story scene and happen before and after the scene like before.)

NATIVE NATION PROJECT

City Card Group Story—Scene 2

Participants participate in the Activity East: Water. Then ...

IRENE: Hey Edward! I've been looking for you. You OK?
EDWARD: Yeah. Sorry I took off. That guy was really bugging me.
IRENE: Random white guys bug me too. I just brought up the Ira Hayes parade because growing up going to it in Sacaton and seeing how the vets were treated, the way they had everyone's respect, that's why I signed up for the army. I wanted that respect you know?
EDWARD: Yeah, I didn't. All my uncles were in the military and they scared me. They weren't mean or anything, just old-school, stern Indian uncles. You know?
IRENE: Yeah, I had those uncles and aunts too. So why'd you go in?
EDWARD: Honestly I looked at all my uncles and they looked like SpongeBob. You know, square body without a butt on top of skinny legs, and I thought, I don't want to look like that.
IRENE: You signed up for the Iraq War to stay in shape? Join a gym.
EDWARD: I know. I guess it was just always assumed that I would enlist one day. I didn't want to at first, but once it was time, I just signed up without thinking about it.
IRENE: I wanted to be a soldier. I wanted that respect the old-timers got.
EDWARD: Do people give you that respect? For being a vet?
IRENE: Not every day. I don't really talk about it. So people don't know.
EDWARD: But you were a big hero with the medals and everything. People gotta know, but they don't care. And that's the truth.
IRENE: Sorry I haven't seen you. Your mom said you moved to the city when you got back.
EDWARD: You could say that.
IRENE: Well, welcome home, Marine.
EDWARD: Thanks. I'm living in my mom's garage.
IRENE: Oh. She made it into an apartment?
EDWARD: I can't sleep indoors. With the big door rolled up ... it's not so bad.
IRENE: Have you talked to anyone about it?

EDWARD: I got a bad back from Iraq. Not lucky like you with a bullet, but an injury from a vehicle wreck. There's no medals for messing up your back trying to avoid a goat. They gave me a lot of oxy. All my life my mom worried it was gonna be meth that put me on the streets. Instead it was a doctor's prescription like a rich white lady in the suburbs.

IRENE: I didn't know you were on the streets.

EDWARD: No one does. No one wants to. You know how many of us are out there? How many "warriors" are out there trying to survive? How many are being kicked off the train in 120-degree heat to die on the pavement?

IRENE: A lot.

EDWARD: Yeah. A lot.

IRENE: I'm sorry.

EDWARD: Not your fault.

IRENE: Come with me to the veteran's center and meet some people.

EDWARD: No thanks. The last time I went to the VA it nearly killed me.

IRENE: No, the one on our land. It's just a place for people to get together and talk.

EDWARD: Talk about feeling like a warrior? No thanks.

IRENE: It's not like that. You know those tough aunts and uncles? When I went to the veteran's center I had their respect, but it was different than I thought it would be. They still busted my chops out in the world, but inside I am in a secret brotherhood and sisterhood that can talk about feelings and take care of each other. They'd talk to you too.

EDWARD: I really don't need to talk about it.

IRENE: OK. I should have checked on you sooner.

EDWARD: We weren't that close.

IRENE: At the center they have all the free coffee you want.

EDWARD: Coffee gives me the jitters.

IRENE: Then we've got water. All the water you want. Until Phoenix uses it up and we all die from dehydration.

EDWARD: But the grass will look good.

IRENE: Right up to the end, some good-looking grass. I'm there every Friday.

EDWARD: I should be at the gym instead.

IRENE: You are getting a little SpongeBob-like.
EDWARD: I know. It sucks. Did you know that Ira Hayes drank himself to death? I didn't know that until I got back.
VICTORIA: Hey, have you seen Beatrice?
EDWARD: Who?
VICTORIA: Molly's kid.
EDWARD: I don't know her.
VICTORIA: She's missing and we need to find her. Glasses, long hair. Wearing a shirt with an eagle on it.
IRENE: We're on it. *(To Edward)* Come on.

*(They take off to help.
    The Water activity continues.)*

RAIN CARD GROUP STORY—SCENE 2

The Appreciation or Appropriation skit and activities happen, then Molly joins Henry and Modie at the stage.

MODIE: Hey Molly! Any news on Beatrice?
MOLLY: No one has seen her. *(Spots Mr. Clark)* And we probably won't as long as THAT guy from CPS is around.
HENRY: We've got half the tribe out looking. We'll find her.
MOLLY: Thanks.

(She goes.)

MODIE: At least CPS came during the day. Usually they come at bedtime and grab the kids so the parents can't run. The little ones show up in the homes of strangers exhausted and barefoot with nothing but pajamas. Would it kill them to let them pack a bag? Keep something of home.
HENRY: If they take Beatrice now we may never see her again.
MODIE: Back in the old days a third of Native kids were taken away from us.
HENRY: Well I looked it up and there are still three times as many Native kids in foster care as white kids.

MODIE: Sometimes they need it, but has Beatrice ever been without food or a roof or love with Molly?

HENRY: Never. Sure they live in poverty, but they are surviving. White people abuse their children and get to keep them, but Beatrice is loved and going to be taken from her home again. Don't tell me that system isn't rigged against us.

MODIE: Of course it is. The children *are* our future, take them away and we're screwed. Divide and conquer. It's all part of the same rigged system we've been fighting since the invasion. But I've got to believe that it's gotten better. I have to focus on the wins or I can't take it.

HENRY: We've gotta figure out a way to help Molly better this time. Raise money to get a real lawyer.

MODIE: And to pay for the transportation to town for court.

HENRY: And to compensate for all the days off work.

MODIE: And a phone card.

HENRY: And internet to fill out the forms.

MODIE: Which means she needs a computer.

HENRY: And enough money on top of all that get internet installed. Their place has never had it.

MODIE: The whole neighborhood doesn't have it.

HENRY: And we gotta be sure the electricity stays on. Internet and computers and phones need electricity.

MODIE: And after all that she needs to have enough money left over so the place looks kept up, or they won't give Beatrice back at all.

HENRY: No wonder we don't get our kids back.

MODIE: The tribe should help more.

HENRY: They do what they can with the resources they have. If we had more Native foster families it would solve a lot. When these kids leave us, they not only lose their family, they lose who they are.

MODIE: It's culture shock. When I got to college I was completely lost. I nearly froze to death that first winter because I had never seen a thermostat before. I thought it was just telling me the temperature. Yes I know I'm freezing, thanks.

HENRY: First time I went to town was the first time I'd ever seen running water. I didn't know about flushing the toilet. Got yelled at when I left a big poop in the bowl.

MODIE: People think we are just like them because we live outside of town and can maybe speak English and dress like them, but we are from sovereign, Native nations. People don't understand that even though we are so close, we are a world apart.

(They start to go as Russ arrives.)

RUSS: We've got to help Beatrice escape.
MODIE: Escape? To where?
RUSS: Anywhere is better than letting them take her away.
HENRY: She is a minor child. There aren't many options.
RUSS: I was younger than her when I ran away the first time and trust me, I did better on my own than with any of the foster families I had.
MODIE: We need to work with the system or Molly may never get Beatrice back.
RUSS: The system is set up to take us apart.
HENRY: But you can't put a girl like her on the streets of the city.
RUSS: We sneak her back to the rez. She stays out of sight and no one needs to know.
MODIE: But what about school?
RUSS: She's barely going anyway.
HENRY: This isn't practical, Russ.
RUSS: I'm not talking about practical. I'm talking about survival. I never would have made it if I'd stayed in any of the group homes they put me in. If I find Beatrice first, I'm helping her run.

(Russ takes off.)

MODIE: Russ! Get back here.
HENRY: You get Russ, I'll check in with Molly.

*(They go.
The Appreciation or Appropriation activity continues.)*

Flower Card Group Story—Scene 2

The participants enjoy the Food activity in the west. Sequoia approaches Raeshawn, who has finished her activity.

SEQUOIA: Raeshawn, I need to talk to you about something. With dating. A thing about dating.
RAESHAWN: You mean you and Houston?
SEQUOIA: You've heard about that?
RAESHAWN: It's obvious.
SEQUOIA: I told you, we are just friends.
RAESHAWN: You clearly had bunny ears around the word "friends." You had them just now.
SEQUOIA: I didn't.
RAESHAWN: They were implied.
SEQUOIA: They are always implied.
RAESHAWN: Fine, but that's who you're talking about, right? You and Houston.
SEQUOIA: Don't tell anyone in my family.
RAESHAWN: I wouldn't. They would freak.
SEQUOIA: They would, right? But is that prejudiced? Or racist or whatever?
RAESHAWN: I guess sort of, but that's not our fault. It's the government that forced the race thing on us. Although we agreed to blood quantum for membership. Or at least our ancestors did way back. But don't worry, you're in.
SEQUOIA: Of course I am. I'm a quarter Piipaash and my mom is on the tribal council with your parents.
RAESHAWN: Well, you are a wobbler.
SEQUOIA: Wait, a wobbler?
RAESHAWN: Like you said, you're only a quarter Piipaash and you have that one questionable great-grandfather who could actually be Mexican. If he's not Native, you fall below the membership line. But so far everyone has accepted the paperwork they made for him.
SEQUOIA: So far?

RAESHAWN: I mean, lots of people have been challenged lately. If his paperwork were thrown out, you wouldn't have enough Native blood to stay enrolled. But don't worry, our families won't let that happen.

SEQUOIA: But some people think I shouldn't be in this tribe?

RAESHAWN: I'm just saying, hypothetically you could be out, so it's natural that you're gonna be careful about who you have kids with.

SEQUOIA: I'd think a woman should always be careful who she has kids with.

RAESHAWN: Sure, but the whole blood quantum thing matters. If you had kids with Houston, they wouldn't be in the tribe for sure.

SEQUOIA: Maybe we could lower the required level. Or change to lineage membership.

RAESHAWN: Since the new casino came people are only talking about raising the level, not lowering it.

SEQUOIA: I never really thought about it before.

RAESHAWN: Yeah, but it totally makes sense that you have to think about it now. I mean it's cool to date Houston and all, but you're not going to have kids with him, so why bring the whole family into it? Have fun. I won't say anything.

SEQUOIA: But I may have kids with him.

RAESHAWN: That's stupid.

SEQUOIA: It's love.

RAESHAWN: Is it love to make kids who are always on the outside? Kids who can never be recognized as part of your people?

SEQUOIA: Well—

RAESHAWN: Is it love to end not just your family line, but to end one whole branch of your tribe? We are a small group of people. One good natural disaster or some hearty zombies could almost make us extinct.

SEQUOIA: Yeah, but that's not all on me.

RAESHAWN: Of course it is. It's on all of us. Our ancestors went through hell just to survive and give us this blood. Our own families have given their whole lives to strengthening our people for the future.

SEQUOIA: I know.

RAESHAWN: So you want to make kids who are invisible to everyone, even your own tribe? You know what it feels like to walk down the street and have everyone speak Spanish to you. And then when we say our people's names, Akimel O'otham and Piipaash, they've never heard of them. On our own land! The least we can do is keep the tribe going for another generation and give those kids a chance to have it different than we did.

SEQUOIA: So you're only going to have kids with a tribal member?

RAESHAWN: Sure. Actually a full blood would be ideal.

SEQUOIA: I can't believe you are saying this. You're going to have kids based on blood quantum?

RAESHAWN: A full-blood dad means my line is good for a few more generations.

SEQUOIA: This is crazy. This isn't how our people traditionally became tribal members.

RAESHAWN: Please. Lots of traditional ways exclude people. My friend grew up on Hopi land, speaking the language and everything, but because her mom's Navajo, matrilineal lines say she has to give all that up and be Navajo with her mom. She doesn't get a choice, but that's tradition. You want to end tradition?

SEQUOIA: No, but blood quantum is a white concept imposed on us to make sure we all die off eventually. We can't let them be right.

RAESHAWN: Look, biology is a real thing. If we don't have something that says who we are, then anyone can say they are one of us. Is that what you want?

SEQUOIA: Maybe that should be OK. Maybe if someone really wants to be a part of our people they should be allowed to be.

RAESHAWN: Then we'll be overrun with wannabes wearing fringe jackets and crystals with Indian names and our culture will be a joke at best but probably disappear for good.

SEQUOIA: It can't be right to have kids only based on race.

RAESHAWN: It's not wrong. And it saves our people. I'm not saying just get together with any Piipaash guy. Date, fall in love, be happy.

SEQUOIA: I am dating. I am in love. I am happy.

RAESHAWN: Look, have fun with Houston. But he's not the future of your people. You are.

(Phineas arrives.)

PHINEAS: Beatrice is missing. We need everyone's help to find her.

*(They all rush off to help.
Participants finish the Food activity.)*

Eyes Card Group Story—Scene 2

Cehia, Pauline, and Cece finish the Missing and Murdered Indigenous Women activity. Cathan arrives with Lozen.

CATHAN: Grandma Pauline! We've been looking everywhere for you.
PAULINE: I'm right here. I stopped at the hospital on the way in.
CATHAN: What's wrong?
LOZEN: Are you OK?
PAULINE: Not for me, for your cousin Cehia and the baby she's growing.
CATHAN: Oh. Glad you're OK. Anyway . . .
CEHIA: We're both fine. Thanks for asking.
CATHAN: I'm glad you and the baby are fine too, Cehia.
LOZEN: Did you find out if it's a boy or girl?
CEHIA: It's way too early for that. But we are hoping for a girl!
CATHAN: Did you hear about Luanne?
CECE: Maybe we should stop on the way home tonight? We can bring her some food.
PAULINE: She needs rest. We will go by tomorrow. I'm sure her parents want a little time together as a family.
LOZEN: She doesn't live at home.
CECE: Her parents kicked her out.
CEHIA: Just like mine when they found out I was pregnant.
PAULINE: Where is she living?
CEHIA: She was with her grandma, but it's so far from town and they don't have a car.
LOZEN: She was missing a lot of school and Luanne loves school.
CECE: So weird.
CEHIA: I love school.
CECE: If I had gotten knocked up like you, I would have happily stayed home and skipped high school.
CEHIA: And do what? I'm not going to live with my grandma the rest of my life.

PAULINE: You are always welcome. All of you kids always have a home with me.

CEHIA: We know, and if Grandma Pauline hadn't taken me in when I got kicked out, I would have been another dropout mom trying to survive. But now I get to have my kid and my dream to go to college and be a teacher.

PAULINE: I'm so proud of you, Cehia. But if Luanne isn't with her grandmother, where was she living?

LOZEN: She crashes with different people.

CECE: Last week she was staying with some kids at that old, abandoned place on the highway turnoff.

PAULINE: That's not safe. Especially for a girl like her.

CATHAN: Exactly! We need to do something.

(Omari and Damian arrive.)

OMARI *(To Cehia)*: We've been looking for you.

CATHAN: Your baby mama had to go to the hospital Omari. Did you know that?

OMARI: Yeah, Cehia is my girlfriend so I went to the hospital with them.

CATHAN: Oh. Well she's fine.

OMARI: I know.

DAMIAN: Why did you tell us all to meet here, Cathan?

CATHAN: Because I'm sick of going to a funeral every weekend.

CECE: We all are.

DAMIAN: I went to two last week.

CATHAN: Luanne tried to be the third. We need to do something radical to change things back home.

OMARI: You keep saying that, but what do you mean?

CATHAN: Did you see how much attention those climate-strike kids got? It was huge.

OMARI: But there were thousands of them.

CATHAN: You have to start somewhere. Protests and marches get attention now. Especially with high-school kids organizing them. We put you, Damian, Lozen, and Cehia in the front of the march.

DAMIAN: Technically, since I don't have a car, I march every day.

CECE: Me too.

CATHAN: Or, even better, we should arrange a protest at the next ceremony. A big one.

DAMIAN: You want to make every Indian in the country hate us? Protest a ceremony.

CATHAN: But they would hear us.

CEHIA: Hear us saying what?

CATHAN: That it's not OK to exclude trans people from ceremony.

OMARI: To be fair, they didn't exclude her. They said she had to dance with the men.

CATHAN: But she's not a man. And if they don't want to respect us, we won't respect them.

LOZEN: But we have to respect them. They are our elders.

CECE: And our cultural leaders.

DAMIAN: And our grandparents.

CEHIA: And how does making everyone mad help? I've got enough people against my dreams because of this baby.

OMARI: Yeah, it's just making more enemies. Elder enemies.

CATHAN: Some old people aren't elders. They are just old. Right, Grandma?

PAULINE: Don't drag me into this.

CATHAN: But you are in this more than anyone. It's because of you teaching us that being Two-Spirit is special that I had the courage to come out to my parents. You are the first place Cehia went when she got kicked out, because she knew you'd take care of her. And I know Damian and Cece have stayed with you more than home when their parents were partying. Lozen is the activist in school she is because you inspired her to use her voice. Omari, I don't know, you're fine, but Grandma Pauline is taking care of your girlfriend and kid so we're all connected through her. If we have your support, Grandma, the other elders will listen.

PAULINE: Think it through. What does this protest look like? What does it accomplish?

CATHAN: We would need more people than just us.

LOZEN: I manage the school-council social media accounts.

CATHAN: If you post about it, we'll be stopped before we get started. This has to stay underground.

CECE: So we hit people up directly. It's not like we don't know every young person on the rez.

CATHAN: We also need to pick the right ceremony. A big one.
DAMIAN: Tasha's coming out is in two weeks.
CATHAN: That's perfect. Her dad is running for council.
LOZEN: She'd be really upset if you messed up her ceremony.
CECE: Yeah. Let's do it.
OMARI: That's not cool.
CECE: She nearly ruined mine.
OMARI: She was a little kid then.
CECE: But she liked messing it up. I could tell.
CEHIA: She always has to be the center of attention.
CATHAN: Says the person who mentions being pregnant every thirty seconds.
CEHIA: I am growing a new human being. That's a miracle.
CATHAN: Yes, we know. You and Omari are miraculous because one night you—
PAULINE: OK, enough. What is your plan, Cathan?
CATHAN: It's not a plan yet. But staging a protest at Tasha's ceremony would get a lot of attention. But it's got to be big enough that they can't ignore it.
OMARI: I'm with Grandma Pauline. This isn't the right way to change things. It will just make it worse.
CATHAN: Grandma is with us. She just said so.
OMARI: No she didn't.
CATHAN: She told us to make a plan.
OMARI: She told you to think it through because it's a bad idea.
CATHAN AND OMARI: Grandma?

(Molly arrives in a rush.)

MOLLY: We are trying to find my niece. CPS came for her and she ran away. We need your help!
PAULINE: Come on, kids. We can make a difference right now. Let's find that girl.

*(They all scatter.
    Participants finish the MMIW activity.)*

TRANSITION 5

Everyone searches for Beatrice, calling for her. A flow of movement bringing everyone back to the center.
  Silence. Time freezes as Beatrice appears on the stage.

BEATRICE: Shhhh. You never saw me. You never saw me here alone, on the run. By trying to stay together I ripped us apart. I've been to their group home. Ten kids in a room. Lights out. Never alone. I can't go back but I don't have a forward to go to.
  You never saw me. There, alone with my mom. Helping her steal to feed us. Helping her steal to get high. Shhh, they don't know. She took the rap for us both. I thought I was alone with her, taking what we needed. Never seen. But now, this is alone.
  You never saw me with my aunt. Getting food and having a bed. She taught me Water Is Life! And No DAPL! She taught me Diné and respect. She taught me to give not take. Now it's all gone. I have nowhere to go. I'm alone.
RUSS: Beatrice!

  (She turns to go.)

This way. Hágo. I'll get you out of here.
BEATRICE *(To the audience)*: Shhhh. You never saw me.

(She runs off with Russ.)

EVENT THREE

Sheerah takes the stage alone.

SHEERAH: An Indian love poem:
 You make me feel like a million food stamps.
 Your breath smells sweet like Shasta.
 You are the jelly on my fry bread.
 Wait, was that my love poem or my shopping list?

I know, things have gotten serious here, but I think it's good to keep a balance while things get settled, so let's go back to our game.

(The contestants join her.)

We last left our contestants in this order, contestant number one is in first place, contestant number two in second, and contestant number three in third place. Here's our next challenge. This one is worth a lot of points. A white couple comes to you at the Magic Butterfly Art Festival—

LORETTA: Why would I go to the Magic Butterfly Art Festival?
DENNIS: I love that place!

LORETTA: Of course you do.

DENNIS: What does that mean?

LORETTA: It means that they created those things for wannabes like you.

DENNIS: I'm not a wannabe.

LORETTA: You are playing the Ultimate Indian Challenge and you're not an Indian.

DENNIS: I've always identified with Native—

LORETTA: But you aren't.

DENNIS: I told you the story.

LORETTA: It's not a story. It's a rumor at best. Most likely a fantasy.

DENNIS: I applied, Sheerah let me in.

SHEERAH: We go by self-identification here.

LORETTA: I challenge that criteria.

SHEERAH: Look, you know it's complicated. We've got Hawaiians and other non-recognized tribes and lost paperwork and people hiding who they were from the bounty hunters and all that. I'm not going to be the Indian police. If people want to play, we let them play.

LORETTA: But why? We're the only people who put up with this stuff. If someone showed up at a Latino event with a sombrero and mustache, they would kick them out, but we take it from these wannabe Indians all the time.

PHINEAS: When you point one finger at somebody, there are three pointing back at you.

LORETTA: What does that mean?

PHINEAS: It means that a degree or two in American Indian Studies at a white college doesn't make you any more Indian either.

LORETTA: Here we go again. Because I didn't grow up on the rez, which as a child I had no choice in, you think I'm not as real an Indian as you.

PHINEAS: You can't have the same view of the world. If you did you may have chosen a less white university to teach you "Indian" studies.

LORETTA: First, I chose my university because my family's medicine man has a degree from it. Second, the emphasis of my degree is in Tribal Leadership and Governance so I can get the skills to go home and serve my tribe.

PHINEAS: You would have done better going home in the first place, participating in ceremony, and asking if they want you to be a leader.

SHEERAH: Let's not turn on each other.

LORETTA: Yeah, that's always our problem, we tear each other down instead of listening to different ways of thinking that may finally make things better on the rez.

PHINEAS: There it is. You city-slicker Indians always look down on us. You pretend you don't, but you do.

LORETTA: Just because I enjoy electricity and running water and iced coffee doesn't mean I look down on people who don't have it.

SHEERAH: That's enough. This is supposed to be a fun game, folks. If you had a problem with self-identification, you should have said something sooner. Now, let's focus back on the game. You're at the Magic Butterfly Art Festival for whatever reason makes you happy. OK?

LORETTA: I could imagine I went to monitor pretend-Indians selling things as Native in violation of the Indian Arts and Crafts Act.

SHEERAH: You do that. Now, here's the deal: a white couple approaches you and says they will pay you one thousand dollars on the spot to give them Indian names. Your challenge is to come up with two names that will make the white people happy enough to give you the one thousand dollars.

PHINEAS: It's not appropriate for me to give them Indian names.

SHEERAH: Come on, you're killing the joke. Two crazy-white-people Indian names. We all know them. It's a game, play with me.

(Everyone thinks a moment.)

OK, contestant number one. What have you got?

PHINEAS: Fire Eagle Crystal and Howling Wolf Woman.

SHEERAH: Not bad. Not bad. OK, contestant number two. What do you have?

LORETTA: Ummm... Thunderbird Waterfall Warrior and Magic Butterfly Dancer. *(To Dennis)* Or did you already get that name at the last festival?

SHEERAH: That's enough. Contestant number three, what's your answer to get the one thousand dollars?

DENNIS: I don't know about the one thousand dollars but the most impressive Indian names I can think of are Deb Haaland and Nathan Phillips.

SHEERAH: Oooooo. We have a winner. Ten points for using current events. That puts contestant number three in the lead.

PHINEAS: You've got to be kidding.

LORETTA: This is so typical. We let these people come into our lives and out-Indian us just because they learn stuff online.

DENNIS: You don't know me. I plant a three sisters garden every year and taught myself to dance pow wow. And when I came to Arizona, I built a wickiup in my yard. Yes, I taught myself all that from books and the YouTube, but technically that was way harder. You had grandparents that just gave you culture. I had to find mine.

At ceremony I do all the hard jobs no one wants. And I put up with people like you making fun of me even though I was there before everyone and stayed after. I proved myself and earned every scrap of knowledge anyone finally agreed to give me. And if this is the end of the third round of the Ultimate Indian Challenge, then I win. I'm the Ultimate Indian because I earned it.

(Dennis grabs the prize and goes.)

LORETTA: This could not be more metaphorical. The white person claims the prize.

SHEERAH: You can't just take it. I have more challenges. More jokes.

LORETTA: I'll get it.

PHINEAS: It's my prize. You're in third place after the wannabe.

(Phineas and Loretta take off after Dennis. A whole line of cast members chase after them.)

SHEERAH: Wait! What about the ceremonial awarding song?

ACTIVITY ROUND THREE

SHEERAH: While they take care of that situation, it's time for the rest of us to rotate to our next activity. You get to try a little of everything at Native Nation.

You know how this works. For this round the eyes, go east. The card with the flowers should head north. Raindrops to the west, and the city folks go south. Get moving to join your third-round activity.

City Card Group Story—Scene 3

The Appreciation or Appropriation skit and activity begin.
Irene and Edward spot Chief at the little stage.

CHIEF: Irene, over here.
IRENE: Hey! Edward, you remember Chief.
EDWARD: Yeah.
IRENE: She's not just a vet, but also an apprentice to a medicine woman back on her reservation. She's legit traditional.

CHIEF: I wasn't always. When I was overseas I missed Mom's fry bread so much, I called her at home to get her to tell me how to do it, but we had a bad connection. So I'm in this guy's room, trying to impress him with my Indian ways, and I mix up the dough and everything and I guess I didn't hear her quite good because it came out like fried crackers. And doing it really smoked up the room. The fire alarms went off and we had to evacuate the whole building!

EDWARD: Did you get in trouble?

CHIEF: Yeah, but it was worth it to have something feel like home. I didn't do so good over there. Got into drinking.

EDWARD: Oh. So this is an intervention?

CHIEF: No, it's just some jarheads and an Army chick sharing stories. But here's the truth, I had problems way before I went into the Marines. Passed down trauma and some hard things in my life. After the Marines I came home an alcoholic and did some bad things.

EDWARD: I've done some things I'm not proud of.

CHIEF: I ended up in jail and I deserved it. Of course I didn't think so at the time. I was smarter than everyone else there. I didn't belong. Then one day, when I was sitting there thinking how stupid these prisoners were, I suddenly had an epiphany: you are the company you keep. That means I'm stupid too. I decided to change my company. Which is hard, 'cause I was in jail with limited choices. But I decided to go to church, and before I knew it, every night at lights out we would hold hands across our cells and pray together. That saved me. When I got out I joined up with my brother. He leads the sobriety group every Friday at his church and I go and help him.

EDWARD: I thought you said you're a medicine woman?

CHIEF: In training. It takes a long time. But my mentor is a medicine woman and a deacon. What I'm trying to tell you is that you don't have to be defined by one thing. Things can be both good and bad.

EDWARD: I feel like I should feel different than I do all the time. I'm here. I survived. I should feel, better.

CHIEF: Naw. You gotta feel what you feel. It's not easy. But you shouldn't do it alone.

(Edward seems to be listening, then suddenly shuts down.)

EDWARD: Where do you get off thinking you are so much better than me?
IRENE: I just thought she could help, as a fellow Marine and—
EDWARD: A drunk? I got addicted because I've got real, physical pain. Not because life is hard or I wanted to run away from home.
CHIEF: We're just talking here.
EDWARD: I keep telling you, I don't want to talk. Leave me alone.

(Edward takes off.)

IRENE: Sorry. I thought he was ready to listen.
CHIEF: We gotta keep trying. I think we better keep an eye on him.

(They go.
   The Appreciation or Appropriation activity continues.)

Rain Card Group Story—Scene 3

The Food activity happens with Molly in the group. Mr. Clark returns.

MOLLY: Did you find Beatrice? Did you send her away already?
MR. CLARK: I didn't find her. Are you sure Beatrice doesn't have a phone?
MOLLY: We share a phone and like I said, it's out of minutes.
MR. CLARK: This isn't good.
MOLLY: You're telling me? My niece is missing in a town she doesn't know and afraid to come back because of you.
MR. CLARK: I'm sorry, but I tried to do this at your home. Does she know anyone around here?
MOLLY: There are cousins in town, but we haven't heard from them in years. They leave and the world swallows them up. Everyone else we know from home is here at Native Nation. Beatrice is most likely to come back here.
MR. CLARK: Then we'll wait.
MOLLY: Yes, she is a good kid. Beatrice's never run away before.

MR. CLARK: Her file says differently.
MOLLY: Not since she's been with me.
MR. CLARK: I can start paperwork while we wait.
MOLLY: If it will help keep my niece, please do it.
MR. CLARK: It is not to change my mind, but to start the process.

(Hillary approaches.)

HILLARY: Excuse me, but my husband and I are Native. Well I am, and I was adopted out of the tribe. My birth parents were addicts too and couldn't care for me so I totally understand. My name is Hillary and—
MOLLY: You mean they suffered substance abuse like my brother?
HILLARY: Anyway, we wanted to give another kid the same chances I had so we are in the process of becoming a foster-to-adopt family.
MOLLY: Beatrice has a family.
HILLARY: I know. We aren't done with the process yet, but since we are in the system, maybe there is a way we could take Beatrice for now?
MR. CLARK: I appreciate your offer, but I'd have to look into the status of your application before I could even consider this possibility.
HILLARY: Can we do that today?
MR. CLARK: I can try.
HILLARY: On a computer or something?
MR. CLARK: Do you know your application numbers?
HILLARY: Yes, I have it all in my tablet.

(Hillary pulls out their phone and gives it to Mr. Clark, who steps aside to figure it out.)

MOLLY: Who are you again?
HILLARY: We were both at Standing Rock? And I've seen you at other environmental actions.
MOLLY: Who's your family?
HILLARY: I don't actually know them since I was adopted. I know it's weird to approach you at such a stressful time, but I thought at least you'd know that Beatrice is in a Native home.

MOLLY: Sort of Native.

HILLARY: My husband is an ally. He's always been supportive of me learning about my culture. He has been to tons of pow wows and marches and events.

MOLLY: I wasn't talking about him.

HILLARY: Oh. I am enrolled.

MOLLY: Having a card doesn't make you an Indian.

HILLARY: Well, it actually does. Legally. And although I missed out on a lot growing up in the city, I had different opportunities I could offer to Beatrice.

MOLLY: Look, I don't need an "enrolled" city slicker telling my niece how much better off they would be if they'd just been taken from their family and moved off the rez like you.

HILLARY: It doesn't hurt to try things that aren't available on the reservation.

MOLLY: Like what?

HILLARY: Umm . . . violin lessons, ballet classes, prep school that prepared me for a top university. I also learned how to be successful in the dominant culture.

MOLLY: Beatrice knows how to dance our dances and sing our songs. She has done all of the proper ceremonies to become a full member of our people. She is learning our language. Those are the things that make us part of the people. Not a piece of paper that tells your blood quantum.

HILLARY: But we also need blood. Biology is a fact, it's not something you can pretend doesn't exist.

MOLLY: Look lady, if you think fighting with me is going to get you my niece, you're wrong.

HILLARY: I'm not trying to take Beatrice. I swear. I just want to help.

MOLLY: You have no idea what it is like to have a community. Your own people surrounding you. To hear your language and know that you are the only people on the planet who can speak to each other in that way. When I grew up, messed up as my family was, I knew I always had somewhere to go for food or shelter. I could go to Henry's home or my grandparents or my auntie down the road or a camp at ceremony and I would be fed and taken care of. Here in this bilagáana town, where will Beatrice go when she needs help? When she is hungry? That's what you're having her give up to live with you.

HILLARY: You're right, I don't know what it's like to have a community like that, and I would love to have it. I've tried to go "home." But no one lets me in.

MOLLY: I'm sorry for that.

HILLARY: I know you feel like I'm against you, but I'm just offering to help you out.

(Mr. Clark returns.)

MR. CLARK: Good news. It looks like Hillary and her husband are qualified for an emergency placement. When we find Beatrice, I can try to get her placed with them ASAP.

MOLLY: You'll try? Where will she be before that?

MR. CLARK: A group shelter. That's standard for a teen. But if you agree to Hillary as a guardian—

MOLLY: No. All of this is still trying to take my niece away. I want her home and that's what I'm going to fight for.

*(Molly goes.
The Food activity continues.)*

FLOWER CARD GROUP STORY—SCENE 3

Ana leads the MMIW activity. Then Houston address the group.

HOUSTON: I hate to interrupt but is there anyone here who is an enrolled tribal member? I'm really struggling with a problem.

VICTORIA: What's going on, Houston? Maybe I can help.

HOUSTON: Thanks, Victoria. I'll just cut to the chase. My girlfriend's an Indian and I'm not and apparently if we have kids together they won't be tribal members.

VICTORIA: Oh, you mean Sequoia?

HOUSTON: We thought it was a secret.

VICTORIA: Not really.

HOUSTON: Does her family know?

VICTORIA: No, her family is intentionally clueless.

HOUSTON: Well that seems to be part of the problem. I didn't know it mattered so much that I'm not Native.

VICTORIA: Some people are real strict about intermarrying.

HOUSTON: Are you?

VICTORIA: No. I'm a sucker for love.

HOUSTON: Does your tribe have this blood quantum thing?

VICTORIA: Yeah.

HOUSTON: You are a member of your tribe, right?

VICTORIA: Yup. Grew up on my reservation.

HOUSTON: Do you miss it?

VICTORIA: Every day. But it's not the right place for me anymore. Had to leave to get a good job.

HOUSTON: Then would it make a difference to you if you weren't enrolled? You're raised that way, but never got the card. Would it change anything?

VICTORIA: It changes everything.

HOUSTON: I don't get that. I have a family and I've always identified as part of my community, but apparently it's not the same thing as a tribe.

VICTORIA: It's more than the people. There is a place on this Earth that has always been ours. Our DNA is connected to this piece of the planet. We could be anyone, but the land makes us who we are.

HOUSTON: I've never felt that.

VICTORIA: I feel it every time I'm with my tribe on my land. I don't know who I would be without that connection.

HOUSTON: That's deep.

VICTORIA: It is.

HOUSTON: So if your kids couldn't have that, it would matter to you.

VICTORIA: It would matter to everyone. Hey, Tama! Come here and help this guy.

(Tama joins them.)

Tama here isn't enrolled but grew up on his rez with his mom. Look, I'm just gonna speak truth, he was never white enough and not Native enough either. He grew up in the culture and speaking the language, but since he's not enrolled he couldn't go to the clinic on the rez. Had to be taken to town.

TAMA: It's true.

VICTORIA: Tell him the park story.

TAMA: After we got the casino, things got real strict with security to keep people out of the residential side of our land. We were like ten, playing in the playground down the street. So two tribal cops stop us and tell me I have to go home. I tell him my mom knows where we are. But they say it doesn't matter, this playground is for tribal members only. If I want to be here I have an enrolled adult with me. Grew up there all my life but in one moment I was no longer one of my own people.

I went away to boarding school in high school and never moved back.

VICTORIA: But you're at ceremony every year.

TAMA: With someone as an escort.

HOUSTON: That's horrible.

VICTORIA: That's blood quantum. It's not perfect, but it's what we have.

HOUSTON: Do you think that's what my kids with Sequoia would have?

VICTORIA: If they're lucky. Some people don't join in as much as Tama did. They just float along the edges like ghosts.

HOUSTON: I don't want that for my kids.

VICTORIA: No one does, but it's what happens. Or you can raise them off the reservation.

HOUSTON: So to have the possibility of happy kids I'd have to move Sequoia away from her huge family that is all IN her life? She'd resent me forever.

TAMA: Maybe.

HOUSTON: So there's no good option.

VICTORIA: I guess not. Do you really need to have kids?

HOUSTON: Yeah. I love kids. So does Sequoia.

TAMA: Then, it's gonna be a thing.

HOUSTON: Why didn't she tell me this sooner?

VICTORIA: I think she really likes you.

HOUSTON: So what would you do?

TAMA: You gotta find your own path.
HOUSTON: Victoria? Come on, you're the one who believes in love.
VICTORIA: I'm sorry, Houston, but maybe love isn't enough here.

(Unseen to Houston, Sequoia arrives.)

HOUSTON: So I need to break up with Sequoia. That's the right thing to do.
SEQUOIA: You just said you wanted to marry me.
HOUSTON: I did.
SEQUOIA: Did?
HOUSTON: But Tama and Victoria explained to me—
TAMA: I think someone needs me somewhere.

(Tama flees.)

SEQUOIA: Victoria?
VICTORIA: I voted for love. At first. But, it's confusing.
SEQUOIA *(To Houston)*: I can't believe you're talking about this with them. You want to break up? Fine.

(She goes.)

HOUSTON: Sequoia wait! That's not what I want.

(Houston goes as Ana leads more activities.)

Eyes Card Group Story—Scene 3

Cehia and Omari do Water activities. When Cehia goes to move a bucket of water . . .

OMARI: Hey! You shouldn't be lifting that. Not while you're pregnant.
CEHIA: That's the point of all of this. Native women have to carry this water and their kids and everything else.
OMARI: Yeah, but you don't have to because I'm here. And I will be here for both of you. I didn't have a dad, but I'm going to be one for our baby.

CEHIA: What about when I go to college?
OMARI: I'll get a job in town and go with you. We're in this together.

(Cathan, Damian, Lozen, and Cece join.)

CATHAN: I've got it! I think we should use this Beatrice thing in our protest. If they don't find her she'll be a Missing and Murdered Indigenous Woman and maybe get some media attention. We tie in to that. "Save Beatrice!" We'll make signs.
DAMIAN: But we don't even know her.
LOZEN: All women matter, if we know them or not, Damian.
CECE: We've got girls we know who need help back in TO. We should be making a "Give diapers to Cehia!" sign.
CEHIA: Shoot, I'd take those diapers.
OMARI: If this protest is a fundraiser for my kid, I'm in. Baby stuff is expensive. I'm working full time on top of school to save up.
DAMIAN: At least you have a job.
CECE: Yeah, Omari, not everyone has an uncle with a business to hire them.
CATHAN: This is a protest. Not a fundraiser.
CECE: But it could be both.
CATHAN: Raising money for diapers is not going to get us attention. We have real issues to put a spotlight on, like for gay and trans people.
CEHIA: Teen pregnancy is a real problem when we don't support the moms or make it so they can finish school. We're trying to beat the statistic.
LOZEN: We started this whole protest idea because we wanted to support Luanne and talk about the suicide issue. It's getting worse every year. That's what we need to focus people on.
DAMIAN: But if there was less drinking—
CECE: And drugs.
DAMIAN: A lot of these problems would go away. We should focus attention on that.
CEHIA: Omari and I don't drink.
CECE: No one said you do.
CEHIA: But Damian implied that stopping drinking would change the issues teen parents face.

CECE: It is a contributing factor a lot of the time.
OMARI: That's what I started with, healthy living. We teach people to live clean and take care of themselves. Like we were just learning about over there.
CATHAN: Healthy living isn't a protest, it's a cause. And we can't protest about alcohol and drugs and everything else or people won't know what we are protesting. I say we stick to gay and trans issues. We protest the treatment Luanne got—

(It falls apart into an argument, everyone fighting for their own cause.
    Grandma Pauline arrives.)

PAULINE: What is going on?!? Is this your protest? Because it's disruptive but I don't see your point.
CATHAN: That's what I'm trying to tell them, Grandma Pauline.
OMARI: I'm telling them that there are too many issues, and the whole protest thing is a bad idea.
CECE: Protesting is hard.
CEHIA: I'm done. Babe, the baby is hungry, can we go eat?
CECE: I want to get one of those tank tops we saw before she sells out.
CEHIA: She makes baby onesies too.
CECE: We have to get you one!
LOZEN: Cece, you can't just go shopping. What about Luanne?
CEHIA: I care, but we've got our own problems. Omari and I gotta focus on our baby.
OMARI: Exactly. Let's go.

(They start to go.)

PAULINE: Get back here. I hoped you kids would work this out on your own, but here's what you're going to do.

(She hands the kids a list.)

This is a list of what you need to get a tribally funded organization established. I suggest you start by holding ceremonies, not disrupting them.

CATHAN: But the ceremony is the whole problem that started this.
PAULINE: People need to feel connected to something bigger than themselves. Ceremony is the way our people did that.
LOZEN: But the elders won't let us do it the way we want to.
PAULINE: Certain elders won't, but believe it or not, all elders are not the same. We have different ideas and ways of doing things, just like you.
CATHAN: We know you're different, but the other elders? They aren't like you.
PAULINE: I have friends. And if you were a group of young people who seemed worthy and asked them in the right way, I am sure my friends would support you in doing a ceremony that was inclusive of all of our ways, old and new.
LOZEN: Luanne could dance with the girls?
PAULINE: I didn't make that new dress to hang in her closet.
OMARI: That's going to make some people mad.
PAULINE: You can't live your life trying to predict how other people react. That's why we have our culture and traditions. Not to control people, but to show them a good way to live.
CECE: Can't we just have the ceremony and not do all of this other stuff?
PAULINE: Sure you could, but what I hear is that you want to make real change back home. That's going to take organization and work and some money. This is how you get that.
LOZEN: But what is our organization about? We can't agree on one thing to protest.
PAULINE: Then make it about all of it.
CEHIA: That's too much. And that's the one thing we do agree on.
DAMIAN: Adults have been trying for generations to solve all those problems.
PAULINE: So if one person tries something and can't do it, no one should ever try again?
DAMIAN: I guess not.
PAULINE: You can do better than that, Damian.
DAMIAN *(Ad-lib)*: You're right, Grandma. Grandma is right, guys! We can do this!
LOZEN: We'll get the leaders from the student council involved.
CEHIA: And the teen mom group.

OMARI: I'll bring other young people who volunteered to plant a community garden.

CATHAN: And I'll bring my Two-Spirit group. And Luanne. She didn't have a group, but she does now.

LOZEN: And you'll help us with the ceremony?

PAULINE: First I'll sponsor your organization request at the council meeting.

CEHIA: We need a name.

LOZEN: What do you think it should be, Grandma Pauline?

PAULINE: It's not my group. It's yours.

CATHAN: But the right way is to get the advice of our elder.

PAULINE: You come up with something and then I'll give my two cents.

(They go.
The participants finish the Water activity.)

TRANSITION 6

A calling-together. A joyous bringing people "home" to the center stage.

Home is more than a place. It's a feeling. It's the one place I can be free.

Home is hauling water and cutting wood. There's something about doing good work. It connects you to each other and the land and nature and history and creator in a way that I just don't feel as strongly as anywhere else but home.

Home is where I had ceremony and my grandpa blessed me.

The air smells different.
Like sheep poop.
And dogs.
Fry bread.
Burning wood.
Red dirt.
Pine trees.

NATIVE NATION PROJECT

Home is where my people are.

The place where I'm not invisible.
Where I'm not a statistic.
Where I'm seen.
Where I can be me.
It's where my heart is.

We are home.

EVENT FOUR

Dennis rushes onto the stage with the trophy. Everyone scatters. Phineas and Loretta close in from both sides.

DENNIS: It's mine!
LORETTA: There's nowhere to go, wannabe.
PHINEAS: You're tall but I'm rez. Skoden!

> *(They run at the stage and fight over the trophy.*
> *People move to intervene, including Sheerah, Sequoia, and Houston. Sequoia and Houston find themselves on stage in the middle of it.)*

SEQUOIA: Stop!
HOUSTON: It's just a game.
DENNIS: Not to me!
PHINEAS AND LORETTA: Me neither!

> *(Henry joins them.)*

HENRY: What is going on?

DENNIS: I won this trophy as the Ultimate Indian.
HENRY: Are you really the Ultimate Indian?
DENNIS: Maybe not the "Ultimate." But I did win the game.
HENRY: Sheerah, is that true?
SHEERAH: Technically, yes.
DENNIS: Ha!
SHEERAH: But, as the creator of the game, I declare twenty bonus points for Arizona-enrolled tribal members.
PHINEAS: That means I win!

(Phineas snatches the trophy away.)

HENRY: Phineas, I hope you realize now that this silly trophy wasn't worth fighting for.
PHINEAS: It totally was!

(He raises his trophy in triumph as he leaves the stage with a disappointed Loretta and Dennis.
  Henry takes center stage as Houston and Sequoia consider each other.)

HOUSTON: Sequoia, you misunderstood me.
HENRY: Ladies and gentle—

(Henry backs up as they take the stage from him.)

SEQUOIA: I know. I spoke to Victoria.
HOUSTON: Come on, let's talk somewhere else.
SEQUOIA: You know what I'm sick of?
HOUSTON: No.
SEQUOIA: Everyone telling me what to do.
HOUSTON: But I thought—
SEQUOIA *(To audience)*: Hey everyone. I'm Sequoia and I've been secretly dating Houston for a year.
RAESHAWN: That is completely shocking!
SEQUOIA: I've kept it a secret because he's not Native American and apparently, I barely am because of blood quantum rules, so if I have kids with Houston, they won't be able to enroll in my tribe. But I'm not going to let some white policy tell me who I can love.

HOUSTON: Really?

SEQUOIA: I'm in love with this man. And if he still wants to, we are going to get married and have kids because that's what I want for my life.

HOUSTON: Even if our kids aren't enrolled?

SEQUOIA: We will still raise them in their Piipaash culture and hope that their people, my people, accept them. And if they don't . . . I don't know.

RAESHAWN: I'll accept them.

VICTORIA: Me too. I love babies!

HOUSTON: Are you sure, Sequoia?

SEQUOIA: I'm sure. So . . . are we still engaged?

HOUSTON: Yeah we're engaged!

(Cheers all around as they embrace.
Beatrice and Russ make their way to the stage.)

RUSS: Beatrice stop!

BEATRICE: No, Russ. I've got to go back.

RUSS: I'm trying to help you.

(Molly grabs Beatrice into a hug.)

MOLLY: We've been so scared. You had everyone looking for you.

BEATRICE: I'm sorry.

(Mr. Clark comes forward with Hillary.)

MR. CLARK: You did the right thing coming back, but since you are a flight risk, you have to go to a secure group home until we are sure you aren't going to run again.

RUSS: I told you this would happen.

BEATRICE: Please don't put me there. I promise I won't run.

MOLLY *(To crowd)*: I need your help. I'm about to lose my niece. Not over abuse or neglect but because our traditional ways of learning aren't respected by the state. My niece knows more about our people and dozens of other tribes because she was with me at Standing Rock and on the Oak Flat Hike and at the uranium mine protest at the Grand Canyon. But the state says that's not good enough. They say I have to put Beatrice in a white school that mentions Native people ONCE in their whole school career. The main rival school they play in sports has a decapitated Native man's head as their logo.

That is the kind of education that tells our children their lives are worth nothing. That is the kind of education that allows them to throw their lives away through suicide and drugs because thirteen years of education on their own land can't see them.

(Agreement from many characters.)

MR. CLARK: This isn't the place—
EDWARD: Then where is? We never talk about these things. This lady is losing her niece. *(To Sequoia)* She's losing her tribe.
LOZEN: We are losing young people on the rez every day.
CATHAN: Especially trans and Two-Spirit kids.
CEHIA: And we lose teen mothers from school.
EDWARD: We also lose vets. On the street. Like me.
CHIEF: Are you sure you're ready to talk about that now?
EDWARD: I'll need some help, but I'm ready.
MR. CLARK: I'm sorry, but this is a legal matter. The rules are clear.
ANA: Well the rules are different here. This is Native Nation.
HENRY: Look, is anyone here an attorney that can help Molly and Beatrice with this foster-placement situation?
HILLARY: I am.
MOLLY: Of course you are.
HILLARY: And I will get a firm to donate their time to represent you. I promise.
HENRY: OK. That's one thing fixed. In the meantime, Beatrice, are you OK with going to Hillary's home? She has followed all the rules, right, Mr. Clark?
MR. CLARK: Technically.
HENRY: Great. Beatrice?
BEATRICE: I guess I'm OK to go there if Auntie is.
TAMA: I live in town, I can visit her.
MR. CLARK: That's not how this works. She's a flight risk.
LORETTA: I live in town too so I can check on her. Anyone else?

IRENE: I will stand watch.

EDWARD: Me too. We can do some talking.

HENRY *(To Mr. Clark)*: Well, that's a Marine and a decorated soldier, is that good enough for you?

MR. CLARK: It's highly unusual, but . . . yes. She can be placed directly with Hillary if the current guardian agrees.

MOLLY: I want to visit as often as I can, and I will fight to get Beatrice home.

HILLARY: We would happily bring her home to visit too, if you'd let us come.

RUSS: Good for her, but what about all the other kids in foster care who are being raised away from their people?

CATHAN: We don't have an answer yet, but in TO we are starting this new youth organization that's about a lot of issues that put kids into the foster system.

LOZEN: Maybe it could be an intertribal group that coordinates with your tribe and others to keep connected with kids like Beatrice?

CEHIA: We'll keep them connected to their culture and kids on the rez. Like mine.

OMARI: We can invite them to our new ceremony we're going to be holding. Right, Grandma?

PAULINE: Absolutely. You have my support.

CECE: So we are going to "Save Beatrice"?

DAMIAN: We're going to try.

(Cheers all around as the cast scatters, leaving Henry on stage.)

HENRY: OK, this Native Nation thing has been a lot more than we bargained for, but this is why we need to get together like this. Together we are stronger and can fix anything, but it's time to wrap it up. Ana has some final instructions.

ANA: Thanks for coming, everyone. On your way out be sure to pick up any trash. We have to leave the grounds exactly as—

BEATRICE: Wait, we can't just end like that. We made a community here. It's like attending a coming-out ceremony—we are responsible to each other now. We need to finish the circle to make sure we all promise to never let any of us feel alone again.

(Several men appear on stage with rattles. They shake them together and begin a song of blessing.

Cast members lead a simple circle dance around the stage. Everyone is encouraged to join in until the entire audience and cast are all blended together, dancing to the music as one people until the song ends.

The music changes, dance party.

Festival continues.)

END

SUPERHEROES ON NATIVE LAND

Todd London

August 2021. We've been traveling the state commonly known as South Dakota for most of a week, starting in Rapid City, COVID testing every day. Last year, the Sturgis Motorcycle Rally, a gathering of half a million bikers in a state with under a million citizens, became a super-spreader event. There are COVID checkpoints at some reservation borders. "They are under siege again," playwright Larissa FastHorse says. Her comment comes loaded with history—Native populations wiped out by previously unknown diseases brought by white European settlers, some unintentional and some murderously on purpose. Against this backdrop, the guests from L.A.'s Cornerstone Theater Company proceed with care.

We enter the tribally sovereign lands of the Oglala Lakota Nation and make our way—with several stops—through the Pine Ridge Reservation, one of the largest reservations in the US. When we reach the Rosebud Reservation in the south central part of the state, Larissa is finally home. The playwright's Sicangu Lakota family comes from Rosebud. It's a place she loves and cherishes, rife as it is with the emotions of family history and, of course, *history* history. "There's nowhere I'd rather be on the earth, nowhere on this planet," Larissa says. "Unfortunately, my work doesn't live here. I've been working my whole career to get back here."

The story of the making of *Wicoun*, like the play itself, is a story of return—to oneself, to the unique powers—even superpowers—of that self. At the heart of the story is the playwright's homecoming, to the place and people she loves best. A Lakota playwright will create a Lakota play with and for Lakota people on Lakota land.

In late 2019 the project expanded to embrace the Dakota and Nakota, "different bands of the same people," as director Michael John Garcés puts it. The seven different tribes, or "Council Fires," that make up these neighboring nations continue to stress their kinship as well as differences. Over a delicious lunch at her kitchen table—chicken and wild rice soup with boiled squash and bread—Dusty Nelson, a community member on Pine Ridge who recently started a daycare center in her home, reels off friendly Lakota jokes at the expense of other tribes. "There are two types of people," she tells us. "Lakota and people who want to be Lakota."

Wicoun is the most geographically rangy and least urban of the three Native Nation plays. While it will be seen by white audiences in Rapid City and at the Black Hills Playhouse, *Wicoun* is developed *by*, *for*, and *about* Native audiences. Thanks to a leaky rental van and this troupe's stamina, it will be performed *near* them. Between summer of 2019 and 2023 the company will cover thousands of miles, crisscrossing the state, stopping in small towns and rural parts of eight of its nine reservations. (On the final tour, in less than three weeks, Michael logs 3,672 miles driven in his rental car. "I'm an accountant's son, so . . .") The question guiding these community engagement circuits is simple: *What do you want to see?* The most consistent answer: *Our own superheroes.*

Rosetta Badhand-Walker, who plays Elder Superhero, met Larissa and Michael in 2018 when they were in Arizona collecting stories for what became *Native Nation*. She was "intrigued" by the way Larissa listened, documenting the community's concerns. A grassroots advocate to spur action from the Arizona House of Representatives on House Bill 2570, "Establishing A Study Committee on Missing and Murdered Indigenous Women and Girls," Rosetta had never been in a space "where people from the outside . . . genuinely wanted to hear what we had to say."

Wicoun is an origin story, the making of a male superhero named Ahí. We meet Ahí as Áya, a teenage survivor of sexual assault, struggling through a gender transition. Áya's journey toward discovering his power is entwined with that transition. Both threads require Áya to cultivate the bravery, perseverance, and generosity to overcome the world's dangers—"Racism. Drugs. Capitalism . . . Humidity"—and be born anew. But Áya needs help to become the superhero Ahí. Lots of it.

The word doesn't translate directly into English, but, as Larissa explains it, wicoun (pronounced *wich'oon*) means a "way of life"— spiritual, cultural, and physical all at once. In his influential book, *The Lakota Way: Stories and Lessons for Living*, historian and educator Joseph M. Marshall III, also from Rosebud, collects stories exemplifying the "requisite virtues" underlying the Lakota way of life. Several of these virtues come to Áya in the form of superhero teachers, each played by a member of the L/N/Dakota community.

WÓOHITIKE. According to Marshall, Wóohitike translates as "having or showing courage" in the face of life's challenges, i.e. bravery. Also known as Victoria (Vicki) Picotte-Sunbear. For Vicki, who lives on Rosebud, the chance to audition for *Wicoun* starts as a joke. Her father forwards her the link announcing auditions because he knows she's scared of public speaking. "And he's like, hey, you should try this. Ha ha. LOL." Vicki's never acted before, but somehow she knows she wants to do it. A formerly certified nurse's aide and stay-at-home mom with one- and four-year-old daughters, she's never been away from her kids. Also, she's pregnant and will be late in her second trimester during the tour. She has her husband and father's support, and the money from the play will be hugely helpful for the family.

With characteristic moxie (she's her mom's "pillar of strength"), Vicki conquers her own fear and, like her character, "just shows up," Larissa's recalls. "We're like, 'Yeah!'" She lands the part. She is Wóohitike. And she loves being onstage, "to see the way people react and laugh and that I'm causing them joy." Larissa and Michael are "super excited to have a pregnant superhero portraying the strongest person."

WÓWAČHIŊTȞANKE. Generous is Christopher Alexander Piña's Lakota name, given to him by his grandmother, who told him, "It's because you're generous, Grandson, that you keep getting blessed." Generosity, it turns out, is the name of the third superhero, but

Generous/Christopher plays number two: the animal shapeshifting Wówačhiŋtȟaŋke, which means Perseverance. Wówačhiŋtȟaŋke's origin story is a version of Áya's life story, substituting animal transformation for gender change. "As a child, I was different," the superhero explains. "I could not control what kind of animal I was. It scared people, even my own family."

It's easy to understand how, for the Plains Native bands, perseverance would be a necessary virtue. "When resistance ceased to be an option," Joseph Marshall explains, "surviving within the parameters of white control on the reservations was the only choice. There was no other option but to reach deep inside and persevere day in and day out . . . one generation to the next."

Wówačhaŋtognake. Áya's third and final magical assist comes from the superhero with Christopher's name—Generosity (which Larissa elides with another virtue, compassion)—played by his real-life friend, Gina Project Celebrity Mallory. A younger school friend who feels like family, Gina trudged after Christopher through a winter storm to auditions. Born Sicangu Miniconjou Lakota and Sisseton Wahpeton Sioux, Gina was adopted by her grandmother, whom she calls "my mom." Her compassion is especially attuned to the struggles of teenagers and children these days, their "tribulations" from "the drugs, the violence, the alcoholism." Her heart goes out to the suffering of others.

Like most of the cast, Gina identifies closely with her character. "I don't believe in holding onto very many possessions. What I have with me is what I have in life because I give everything and anything away." She and Christopher started a "Regiftmas" one holiday season, giving presents to thirty-two families in Rapid City and Pine Ridge. They provided gifts to one hundred and seventy-two adults, children, and animals. And so arrives Wówačhaŋtognake, who teaches Áya that to be truly generous one must "hold nothing back" and "trust in being provided for."

Still, everything crashes in on Aya. Three superheroes aren't enough. Áya calls on the fourth cardinal virtue, Wóksape, but no one appears. This virtue—*Wisdom* or in Marshall's words, "knowing what to do with what you know . . . "—has to come from within. Before our eyes, as Larissa writes, "Áya makes a grand dramatic gesture to shed the female expression of themself and transitions before our eyes to a trans man, with a little flair that holds their female power, too. It's Clark Kent into Superman. Instant and awesome. We wonder why we didn't always see it." Áya becomes Ahí, arrayed in beautiful regalia.

In a remarkable convergence, an Oglala Lakota singer/songwriter named 9A plays Áya. 9A's "Lakota Pop" has earned her multiple honors from the Native American Music Awards and 17,000 Tik-Tok followers. Her quest mirrors Áya's in many ways, including the deepening connection to Lakota values. She grew up in Humboldt, Iowa, where her Lakota mother and aunt had been "adopted out" in infancy to a white Catholic family. Her grandparents, having traveled the world as missionaries, had a greater tolerance of cultural difference than many who "scooped" children out of Native communities. Before her twenty-first birthday, 9A moved back to the Pine Ridge Reservation, beginning a journey of emergence, self-reconciliation, and healing. Transitioning to a man onstage and a woman in life, "It's sort of beautiful how I'm reconciling my transness and figuring out being Oglala Lakota." The message is simple and profound: if people can change, so can the world.

I wish I could convey the power of watching a play with the audience that helped create it and for whom it is precisely intended. Whether it happens in a gymnasium or parking lot, the specific, local, almost genetic connection between story and spectator, actor and role, provides a communal electricity I rarely feel in theater made for more generalized audiences. Even the laughs are different. The first performance of *Wicoun*'s statewide tour in Ft. Thompson, part of the Crow Creek Reservation, brought this truth home. Brandon Sazue's home to be exact.

Hunkpati Dakota, Brandon's a student, along with his twenty-nine-year-old daughter, at Lower Brule Community College. Though he'd never acted before, "I was like, I *can* do this." He took a break from his day job as a school janitor and, because he also drives a school bus, drove it home to audition on Zoom. He had a powerful intuition the play would change his life, aid his recovery from hellish years that began at the Standing Rock protests in 2016. As thousands of Indigenous protestors from dozens of tribal nations gathered to halt the Dakota Access Pipeline that would deliver oil from North

NATIVE NATION PROJECT

Dakota to Illinois, Brandon worked hard at the encampment, driving people everywhere. During a violent and successful police action to break the protests, he was arrested and put into prison. "Everything went to shit after that," he says. "I was so broken." The play, he knows, "is giving me my life back."

The performance takes place on a grassy lot between the Crow Creek Sioux Tribe offices and the hangar-like building where Brandon spent three two-year terms as tribal chairman. Brandon plays three roles: a Meth Zombie, "Native Party Dude," and Chris, a helpful comic book nerd (no superheroes). His performance seems particularly confident. When he's onstage, his twins, who turned four just yesterday, settle and watch him, transfixed. As if that isn't great enough, when we return to the Rosebud Reservation's Quality Inn, he puts a quarter in a slot machine and wins five hundred dollars. "Bringing the theater to Crow Creek, to my hometown . . . it just doesn't get any better than that. We made history. Nobody's ever brought theater to the tribes like this. Ever."

Excerpted from "Superheroes on Native Land," a three-part essay series of the same title originally published on AmericanTheatre.org, in November and December of 2023. Adapted and reprinted by permission of Theatre Communications Group.

TODD LONDON's many publications include two novels and numerous books about the theater: *This Is Not My Memoir* with André Gregory; *An Ideal Theater*; *Outrageous Fortune*; *The Importance of Staying Earnest*; *15 Actors, 20 Years*; *The Artistic Home*; and Zelda Fichandler's *The Long Revolution* (editor). He spent eighteen seasons as Artistic Director of New Dramatists and four years as Executive Director of the University of Washington School of Drama. A past winner of the George Jean Nathan Award for Dramatic Criticism, he was the first recipient of TCG's Visionary Leadership Award for "advancing the theater field as a whole." www.toddlondon.net

WICOUN

*Created through collaboration between Larissa FastHorse,
Michael John Garcés, and people of the Oceti Sakowin*

PRODUCTION HISTORY

Wicoun was commissioned, developed, and produced by Cornerstone Theater Company on tour throughout the Oceti Sakowin in 2023 from May 25–June 16. *Wicoun* was performed at the Black Hills Playhouse, Racing Magpie, and Main Street Square in Rapid City; outdoors at the Great Plains Crow Creek Office in Fort Thompson; Todd County Middle School in Mission; St. Francis Indian School; the First Annual Two-Sprit Powwow at the Memorial Park Bandshell in Rapid City; Red Shirt School; Little Wound School in Kyle; Ground Control Skate Park in Pine Ridge; Lakota Youth Development in Milks Camp; Marty Indian School; the Coliseum of Sioux Falls; Riverside Park Ampitheater in Yankton; Standing Rock CDC Gym in Fort Yates; Steamboat Park Ampitheater in Pierre; and at the Cheyenne River Youth Project in Eagle Butte.

The scenic and prop design was by Nephelie Andonyadis, the puppet design was by Lynn Jeffries, the costume design was by Jeanette TIZAPAPALOTL Godoy, and the sound design was by Talon Bazille Ducheneaux. The Lakota language translator and consultant was Jerome Kills Small; the community advisor and collaborator was Clementine (Minnie) Bordeaux; the rehearsal stage manager was Michael Garcia, the performance stage manager was Maria V. Oliveira, and the assistant director was Sapphire Tiger; the production managers were Geoff Korf and Ash Nichols; and the company manager was Paula Donnelly. The cast was:

ÁYA	9A (Nee-nuh)
ELDER SUPERHERO, ENSEMBLE	Rosetta Walker
ALL THE WAŠIČUS, ENSEMBLE	Peter Howard

WÓWAČHAŊTOGNAKE, ENSEMBLE	Gina ProjectCelebrity Mallory
WÓWAČHIŊTȞANKE, ENSEMBLE	Christopher Alexander Piña
WÓOHITIKE, ENSEMBLE	Victoria Picotte-Sunbear
KHOSKALAKA	Kenny Ramos
ZOMBIE, CHRIS, MARCUS, ENSEMBLE	Brandon J. Sazue Sr.

Community Partners for *Wicoun* included First Peoples Fund, Racing Magpie, Lakota Youth Development, Brave Heart Society, Cheyenne River Youth Project, Cheyenne River Sioux Tribe Title One Program, Black Hills Playhouse, Black Hills Community Theatre, the City of Rapid City, and Lakota culture bearers.

CHARACTERS

Pronouns and gender terms were chosen based on original actors but should be changed as needed to fit future actors. Names also change as needed to reflect gender of the actor.

KHOSKALAKA (or WIWASTE): Teen Lakota man (or woman). Cousin brother to Áya. He is trying to instill Lakota values in the many kids they are raising together, and to graduate high school, but it's hard. High-achieving personality who feels responsible for everyone.

ÁYA: Young Lakota teen with some Dakota ancestors. Cousin sibling to Khoskalaka. Assigned female at birth and still presents that way when needed, but at home they are living in a true Two-Spirit place, often called nonbinary. However, their desire is to transition to male. They keep Khoskalaka from getting too serious about everything.

KID ONE: Native kid.

KID TWO: Native kid.

CHEYENNE: Native teen, trying to do the right thing.

JESSIE: Native teen, interested in some fun.

METH ZOMBIES 1 AND 2: Needs their methicine.

ELDER SUPERHERO: Walks with a walker or cane, takes their time but is super entertaining. They have lots of Elder Power, and cookies.

CHORUS: Folks.

TODD: White guy. Drug dealer looking to score a Native woman so he can take advantage of her land and tax status.

MARCUS: Native party dude. Brother to one of the kids living with Áya and Khoskalaka.

TATÉ: Native party girl who hangs with Todd and Marcus.

WÓOHITIKE: Superhero representing bravery. She has super strength. Funny, confident.

WÓWAČHIŊTȞANKE: Superhero representing perseverance. His power is changing into different animal forms.

OFFICER: Rapid City Police Officer. Not nice.

CHRIS: Dakota elder. Young at heart. Proud superhero nerd.

BUS DRIVER: Native driver of the bus.

BLOW UP THE FACES PERSON: Protester in support of returning the Black Hills to the Oyate.

COUNTER PROTESTER: White person against giving the Black Hills back.

WÓWAČHAŊTOGNAKE: Superhero representing generosity and compassion. Their power is super speed.

OPENING—CHORUS

The chorus sections can be performed many ways. In the original production, the cast circled Áya as they yelled insults at her.

CHORUS: Why do you have to be such a freak?
    What's wrong with you?
    We'll take care of you.
    Watch your back.
    I'm gonna beat you up.
    You shouldn't be allowed to be around children.
    Get out of this bathroom!
    Why can't you be a normal girl?
    Get away from me, fag.
    Don't be a sissy.
    You need a real man to make you a woman.
    Why don't you just kill yourself?

(Chaos of all lines together, then . . .)

(All together) Why don't you just kill yourself?

SCENE I

Khoskalaka and Áya's Home—Main Room

Sounds of night on the reservation: police sirens, people arguing, parties, barking dogs. But we also hear very loud children playing in another room.
   Khoskalaka draws and writes frantically, very stressed. Áya watches, not impressed.

ÁYA: Khoskalaka, you have got to chill.
KHOSKALAKA: It was bedtime twenty minutes ago and I don't have their new comic book ready.
ÁYA: Don't you make up these stories so bedtime is easier, not more stressful?
KHOSKALAKA: And to give them good things. Normal things, Áya.
ÁYA: Normal? Those kids are being raised by two teenagers without an adult in sight.
KHOSKALAKA: Which is why we need to give them normal structures.
ÁYA: There's nothing normal in this house.

KHOSKALAKA: But we can try. It's normal for kids to have bedtime stories read to them by their parents.

(Áya gives Khoskalaka a look.)

ÁYA: And you know this, how?

KHOSKALAKA: OK, not my parents. Or your parents.

ÁYA: Or the parents of any of those kids in there. You spoil them.

KHOSKALAKA: We are all they have left.

ÁYA: But we aren't their parents. They are our siblings and cousins. Except Bradly. I don't have a clue where he came from.

KHOSKALAKA: OMG! I didn't want to admit it but I swear I've never seen that kid before.

ÁYA: I thought you told him he could stay?

KHOSKALAKA: No. I thought he was from your side of the family.

ÁYA: Well, it's been like two weeks and no one has come looking for him.

KHOSKALAKA: What if he's been reported missing?

ÁYA: I'll ask around at town tomorrow, but I haven't seen him on the MMIP Facebook pages, so I think he's ours now.

KHOSKALAKA: That's exactly my point. We are the closest to parents that they've got. I already checked out every kid story they had at the library, and then got fined because we didn't have the gas money to get them back in time. Now I make my own. Besides, mine are better. And no one has drawn dirty pictures in them that we have to explain away.

(They both laugh at the memory.)

ÁYA: Watching your face trying to explain that last one.

KHOSKALAKA: I can never look Mickey Mouse in the face again.

ÁYA: Me either.

KHOSKALAKA: Help me get this done. I have to get them to sleep so I can study. I'm behind and there's a huge test at the end of the week.

ÁYA: What's the story about?

KHOSKALAKA: Zombies. They wander from party to party at night, taking zombie medicine that eats their brains. But instead of them trying to eat you, they get you to take their zombie medicine that eats your brain from the inside out.

ÁYA: Subtle. You should call the medicine "methicine."

KHOSKALAKA: I like it. Now, I need to come up with a Lakota superpower that will defeat the zombies and their methicine.

ÁYA: You know superheroes are not my thing.

KHOSKALAKA: Kids love superheroes. And they are easy to write. Something goes wrong, superhero saves the day, bedtime. So, zombies . . .

ÁYA: Oh, I know the zombie catch phrase . . .

KHOSKALAKA AND ÁYA: Meth, we're on it!

(They laugh again.)

ÁYA: Look, if the Lakota or Dakota or Nakota, I'm sure, had the answer to meth, we would have used it long ago and everything would be different.

KHOSKALAKA: The Oceti Sakowin have lots of answers that we just don't use anymore. I mean, think about the old stories. Our people had real power. Super power.

ÁYA: That's not how things are now.

KHOSKALAKA: Let me have my escape. The point is, we need to find our way back.

ÁYA: I am only interested in forward.

KHOSKALAKA: That's not true. If we were back in the old days, you would not have to hide who you are or choose one way to be. You would be revered for being both winyan and wichasa. You'd be the holiest of holy. So powerful, who knows what you could do? Walk on water! Command the winds!

ÁYA: Today, if I don't look like the girl people want me to be, I get beat up. Or . . . you know.

KHOSKALAKA: We won't let that ever happen again.

ÁYA: You can't promise that. No one can. But if I don't go back home, I'm a little safer.

KHOSKALAKA: This is your home now. Our home. The wasicu call us cousins, but in the Lakota way we are brother and sister. And when you're ready, brothers.

ÁYA: It should be an elder that talks really slowly for a really really long time.

KHOSKALAKA: Huh?

ÁYA: The superhero. Tweakers are all anxious, right? The elder talks them into submission. The more stressed the tweaker gets, the slower the elder talks, until they fall asleep.

(They both laugh.)

KHOSKALAKA: Is that disrespectful though? It's a privilege to listen to our elders.

ÁYA: It's funny. Who has a better sense of humor than our elders?

KHOSKALAKA: OK, but instead of putting them to sleep, the elder will entertain them and distract them. That works. But I don't have time to translate it all into Lakota.

ÁYA: Pretend the elder is from the boarding school era and doesn't know the language.

KHOSKALAKA: Perfect. Sad. But perfect. Color these pages.

(Áya rolls their eyes but joins Khoskalaka.)

ÁYA: Color? These kids should be grateful for whatever they get.

(They finish and Khoskalaka staples pages together triumphantly.)

SCENE 2

Khoskalaka and Áya's Home—Little Kid Bedroom

It's chaos. Kids everywhere.

ÁYA: Bed. Now. Or no story.

> *(A few kids drop into piles all over the room.)*

> Bed in ten seconds or it's no Cheerios for a week. Oatmeal only. Ten. Nine. Plain oatmeal. No sugar.

> *(That does it. The rest drop into their sleeping positions all over the room: on a mattress, in chairs, on the floor, etc.)*

KID ONE: Do you have a new story?
KHOSKALAKA: I do.
KID TWO: Finally!
KHOSKALAKA: Áya helped me with it.

KIDS: Wopila Áya!

(Some kids jump up and get excited.)

ÁYA: Cheerios.

(The kids quickly drop back to sleeping positions. Khoskalaka opens the comic book and everything changes.)

SCENE 3

Bedtime Story—Meth, We're on It

The story is in Lakota and someone runs out with cue cards with the English translation (designated in brackets) as subtitles in a funny way. Or translates like an ASL translator at a show, again comically. Or perhaps the reverse. Don't take it too seriously. A "Meth, We're On It" zombie dance. A teen, Jessie, starts to leave their house at night. The Zombies hide and watch. Cheyenne stops Jessie.

CHEYENNE: Tokiya la he? O'iyokpaza sam iyaye. [Where are you going? It's after dark.]
JESSIE: Unci ti ekta. [Grandma's.]
CHEYENNE: Oye oteȟike. Wičun-t'e naǧi ki . . . [It's not safe. The zombies . . .]
JESSIE: Wa ƙowakpe šni. [I'm not scared.]
CHEYENNE: Taku eč'anu ke'ayeš, thapežuta ki iču šni yo. Ayeš nasula nithawa ki mahel oȟunwin kte. Watohanl nisinya wicun-t'e nagi henica kte. [Whatever you do, don't take their methicine. They

will tell you it's good, but it will rot away your brain from the inside until you are nothing but a zombie too.]

JESSIE: Hau, hau. (Han, han.) [Yeah yeah.]

CHEYENNE: Nihakab mawani kte. [I'm coming with you.]

(They head out. Immediately Meth Zombie 1 comes at them, super-obviously creepy. Jessie and Cheyenne quickly duck and run past them. Easy. Meth Zombie 2 does the Meth Zombie dance; it's fun. Cheyenne and Jessie are interested. This seems OK. They dance a bit with Meth Zombie 2.)

Wicun-t'e nağı ki o'iyokipi yuha pi. [Zombies are funner than I expected.]

(They keep dancing. Meth Zombie 1 pulls out their methicine and takes it. They offer to Jessie, who grabs it.)

CHEYENNE: Aphe yo! [Wait!]

JESSIE: Hanhepi ataya o'iyokipi yuha pi. He wačin. [They have fun all night. I want that.]

(Elder Superhero appears across the playing space. They use a cane or walker.)

ELDER SUPERHERO: Stop!

(Everyone freezes in the presence of Elder Power. Elder Superhero crosses toward them, but comically slowly. They wait. And wait.)

CHEYENNE: Unci/Lala oničiyapi yačin pi he? [Unci/Lala do you need help?]

ELDER SUPERHERO: I've got it.

(Elder Superhero gets their cane or walker stuck.)

Maybe if you could just carry my bag.

(Cheyenne runs over and takes the Elder Bag, a glorified reused plastic bag. They help Elder Superhero get unstuck and walk slowly

beside them. Meanwhile, Meth Zombie 2 becomes agitated; this is taking too long. They need a fix.)

METH ZOMBIE 2: Phežuta wečin. [I need my methicine!]

(They grab it away from Jessie.)

ELDER SUPERHERO: I said stop!

(They all stop again and wait as Elder Superhero walks so slowly.)

I should have entered from the other side.

(They keep walking. Meth Zombie 2 starts tweaking. Jessie is freaked and moves away. Meth Zombie 2 grabs Jessie, shaking and tweaking. Meth Zombie 1 returns, also tweaking.)

They've moved into the tweaks. I will use my Elder Powers to distract them so Jessie can escape. Aye! When I was a young one like you, we didn't have zombies to worry about, but we did not have it easy. At all. We didn't have this indoor plumbing. You wanted water, you had to haul it. And trust me, when you had to carry that water, you were not wasteful. Not with a drop. Oh, and I never saw a flush toilet until I was almost an adult and went to town for the first time. I was never so scared in my life. The noise and the whooshing. I thought it was going to pull me right down with it.

(Elder Superhero suddenly SCREAMS!, terrifying everyone into attention; even the Zombies snap out of it.)

CHEYENNE: Nitanyan he? [Are you OK?]

ELDER SUPERHERO: That's how scared I was! I screamed and shot out of that little coffin-sized bathroom so fast I fell into the arms of some poor white lady, who started screaming too. Then another toilet flushes in the other little room and I'm screaming again and she's screaming, so the store owner comes running armed with a baseball bat, thinking we are being murdered. Poor man can't sort out what is happening. He finally calms the white lady down, and to his credit, doesn't make fun of my ignorance and shows me how the toilet works so I won't be scared anymore.

(Everyone is charmed. Even the Zombies have calmed. Elder Superhero talks gently to them.)

Why don't you give me that methicine and I'll walk you home. I've got some nice cookies here in my bag.

(Elder Superhero has Cheyenne pull out the cookies. Meth Zombie 1 thinks about it, but then Meth Zombie 2 takes a hit of their methicine and takes off. It's too much for the first one; they reluctantly follow. Elder Superhero gives cookies to Cheyenne and Jessie.)

JESSIE: Waskuyeča chin pi sʼelel. [It looked like they wanted the cookie.]
ELDER SUPERHERO: They do. Remember, all zombies were just people once. People we loved. And still do. But that methicine is strong. It kills more than it gives. We don't give up on them just because they didn't take the cookie the first time. Next time they may. If it's not too late. Now let me walk you to your unci.

(The three walk off together.)

SCENE 4

Khoskalaka and Áya's Home—Main Room

KHOSKALAKA: It wasn't my best.
ÁYA: It worked. That's all that matters.

> *(The sounds of the night rise and fall—sirens, fighting, party music—as Áya and Khoskalaka pull out their schoolbooks.)*

I swear, if they wake those kids up . . .
KHOSKALAKA: Most of them can sleep through anything now. Or at least they pretend to.

> *(Khoskalaka opens a schoolbook.)*

I don't believe it!
ÁYA: I don't know why you believe anything in those books. They're all written by white dudes.

KHOSKALAKA: Lala's name is written in the front of my book. That school has been using this same textbook for three generations!
ÁYA: No way!

(They look at the names. It's true.)

KHOSKALAKA: I seriously can't believe it.
ÁYA: This is what I keep telling you, this white-guy school is a waste of time.
KHOSKALAKA: It's not. We are going to be the first people in our family to graduate from high school. I know Lala dropped out to do that relocation-job-training thing in Saint Paul, but we are gonna stick it out.
ÁYA: Was that when he became a plumber?
KHOSKALAKA: No, that was the second time in Denver. In Saint Paul he learned house painting.
ÁYA: Right. Then Portland for the electrical training.
KHOSKALAKA: No one took advantage of the relocation program like him.
ÁYA: It was cool though. I remember his whole street of houses were so nice. The plumbing and electricity worked and they were painted all different colors.
KHOSKALAKA: Now half of them are empty or full of zombies. Garbage everywhere.
ÁYA: Your next superhero story should be a historic one about a guy who uses the relocation program to gather all of his powers from all over the country. Then he comes home and saves everyone from blight.
KHOSKALAKA: That's actually cool.
ÁYA: I know. That's why I said it. You never give me credit.
KHOSKALAKA: I literally just did.
ÁYA: But all surprised, like I don't come up with cool things All. The. Time.
KHOSKALAKA: If you're gonna cry around and be grouchy about it . . .
ÁYA: I hate it when you say that!

(Áya and Khoskalaka physically fight it out, like siblings. Maybe books are threatened. Favorite things taken away. It's physical but not hurtful. They know when to stop.)

KHOSKALAKA: Fine, you win. You say all of the cool things and come up with all of the good ideas all of the time. I'm in awe of the stuff you say. I should keep a journal so I never forget. Now give me Lala's book back. I have to learn this stuff. Unlike you, I need good grades to get college scholarships.
ÁYA: Well, one of us has to stay home with the kids.
KHOSKALAKA: Maybe we could both go to college and bring the kids with us?
ÁYA: We're gonna drag these kids to college? To stay in a dorm? Social services would take them away in a day. And ICWA would send them home to their messed-up family.
KHOSKALAKA: *Our* messed-up family.
ÁYA: So we stick to the plan. I will, for some mysterious reason, finish high school, and you will do tribal college, then go to USD, while I stay home with the kids. Then you will come home, get a real job, and make money for all of us.
KHOSKALAKA: We'll be bougie Natives.
ÁYA: With beaded medallions so big that we can't sit down. We stick to the plan and everything will work out fine.
KHOSKALAKA: And you'll be OK with the kids alone?
ÁYA: Sure. You'll come back on weekends.
KHOSKALAKA: When I can.
ÁYA: What do you mean?
KHOSKALAKA: I mean things come up. You need to be able to care for the kids full time if necessary.
ÁYA: Yeah, sure. I've got the kids.

(Khoskalaka seems to make a decision. He pulls out a piece of paper and starts to unfold it.)

KHOSKALAKA: What if you had to take care of them for a long time? Like longer that a few weeks?
ÁYA: Why? You're coming back right?
KHOSKALAKA: Of course I'm coming back, but what if—
ÁYA: You're going to go away and leave us all alone?
KHOSKALAKA: Not forever, but what about—
ÁYA: You're planning to forget us?
KHOSKALAKA: I couldn't. You're my family.

ÁYA: So what are you going on about?

(Khoskalaka refolds the paper.)

KHOSKALAKA: Nothing. Never mind. I'm just stressed about this test.

(Áya thinks about their own future, and it doesn't look like much.)

ÁYA: Do you believe those old stories?
KHOSKALAKA: The ones we made up?
ÁYA: No, the stories everyone knows. The old ones.
KHOSKALAKA: Unfortunately lots of people don't know them anymore.
ÁYA: You sound like Elder Superhero. You know what I'm talking about. Did they really happen? Just like they tell it? Could we really walk on water and talk to animals and turn men to a pile of bones?
KHOSKALAKA: Some powers were only for special beings, like White Buffalo Calf Woman turning the hunter to a pile of bones. I don't think anyone else did that. But in other stories people went really long distances, like across the whole Earth, and everyone seemed to talk with animals and stuff.
ÁYA: So it really happened? Just like that?
KHOSKALAKA: I think of them more like the Bible. Like Christians believe everything in there is really true. But some also say part of it is actual history and part of it is a story meant to illustrate a real concept or belief or lesson. Like, it's real, and they believe it, but it's not all literal.
ÁYA *(Disappointed)*: Right. It would be cool if it was literal. If we could have powers like that again. Then we'd always feel safe.
KHOSKALAKA: Yeah, and we'd never be hungry.
ÁYA: And we'd dress so cool.
KHOSKALAKA: And we'd all have our own beds.
ÁYA: And our own parents. Good ones.
KHOSKALAKA: I do believe that the old ways can help us. Not in a magical, superhero way, but they can make us stronger to overcome bad things. And teach us real things, like for the environment.

ÁYA: Speaking of the environment, that rally to blow up Mount Rushmore starts tomorrow.
KHOSKALAKA: Now *that's* a fantasy.
ÁYA: It is if we don't try.
KHOSKALAKA: We aren't missing school for a stupid Blow Up the Faces Rally.
ÁYA: Come on. We couldn't make it to Standing Rock. This is our chance to—
KHOSKALAKA: No!
ÁYA: You never want to do any of my stuff.
KHOSKALAKA: *Our* stuff is going to school.

(Áya takes off outside.)

Where are you going?
ÁYA: I can't go for a walk without your permission either?
KHOSKALAKA: Be careful. Zombies.
ÁYA: Lock the door.

(Áya goes. Khoskalaka pulls out the paper from earlier.)

KHOSKALAKA: By the way, I got a four-year scholarship to a college five states away but it may as well be the moon because there's no way I can leave all of you for that long. So no one is getting what they want. Yay us.

(He folds the letter back up and tucks it in his pocket.)

SCENE 5

Chorus Transition—Powerful

The chorus can be performed in many ways. In the original production, some lines were spoken in English, some in Dakota/Lakota, some in both. Generally, Dakota replaces the letter "L" with "D." It's more complicated, but that's a start.

CHORUS:
    I feel powerful when my choices are seen and approved.

    I feel powerful when I am me!

    I feel powerful when I help others.

    I feel powerful when I embrace myself to a T and others match me.

    I feel powerful when I'm at sundance.

I feel powerful on the rez.
Wowas'ake bluha tohanl tiyata oyanke ekta wa'un chanasna.

I feel powerful in the lodge.
Wowas'ake bluha tohanl tipi timahel wa'un chanasn.

I feel powerful when I'm sleeping.
Wowas'ake bluha tohanl mistima chanasna.

I feel powerful when I'm playing video games.
Wowas'ake bluha tohanl naskanskan yapi waskata chanasna.

I feel powerful around other Natives.
Wowas'ake bluha tohanl Lakol oyate wicigna wa'un chanasna.

I feel powerful when I'm alone.
Wowas'ake bluha tohanl misnala wa'un chanasna.

I feel powerful when my family is around me.
Wowas'ake bluha tohanl miti-takuye mihomni un pi chanasna.

I feel powerful off of the reservation.
Wowas'ake bluha tohanl oyanke ihayeb wa'un chanasna.

I feel powerful when I speak my language.
Wowas'ake bluha tohanl Lakol iwaya chanasna.

I feel powerful when my hair is in braids.
Wowas'ake bluha tohanl wesun chanasna.

I feel powerful at school.
Wowas'ake bluha tohanl Owayawa ekta wa'un chanasna.

I feel powerful when I am at my grandma's.
Wowas'ake bluha tohanl Uncila ti ekta wa'un chanasna.

I feel powerful when I take care of others.
Wowas'ake bluha tohanl wawowakiya chanasna.

I feel powerful when I play basketball.
Wowas'ake bluha tohanl tab waskata chanasna.

I feel powerful when I remember I am Lakota.
Wowas'ake bluha tohanl maLakota ki weksuya chanasn.

. . . Dakota.
. . . Nakota.

ALL: Oceti sakowin ki unkiye pi.

SCENE 6

Outside—Wóohitike

Áya walks along the dark road. They are lost in thought and don't notice a couple guys and a woman cutting across the prairie toward them. One, Todd, is a white guy. Marcus and the woman, Taté, are Native.

TODD: Áya, wait up.

(Áya is startled by them and instantly on guard.)

ÁYA *(To themself)*: If there are superheroes, I could use one right now.
TODD: We are heading to your place. Is your little man home?
TATÉ: Is he a man?
MARCUS: That fairy?
ÁYA: Leave Khoskalaka alone.
TATÉ: Or is the man you?
TODD: Should I check?
ÁYA: Stop it.

MARCUS: I wanna see my little brother.
ÁYA: They are kids. They're asleep.
MARCUS: So I'll wake him up. I haven't seen him in weeks.
ÁYA: Come back in the morning. When you're . . . better.
MARCUS: I'm just fine. In fact, I'm really good. You should try this stuff Todd made.
TODD: We'll have a private party at your place.

(They keep walking toward the house. Áya points in the other direction.)

ÁYA: You want a party? Come on. Let's head down the road. They've been partying all night.
MARCUS: Shayla's? I can't go there. Got in a fight with her snag.
ÁYA: He's gone. Come on. It'll be fun.
TODD: You gonna make it fun?

(He grabs Áya's shoulder. Áya cringes but leaves it there.)

ÁYA: Just come with me to Shayla's.

(They turn around.
Suddenly Wóohitike appears. They are clearly not of this world. Their power is super strength.)

WÓOHITIKE *(To Áya)*: You called?
ÁYA: Who are you?
WÓOHITIKE: Wóohitike, of course. Watch.

(Wóohitike lifts Marcus over their head and spins them around, WWE-style.
Taté knows when to run, and runs.)

To be clear, I could throw you all the way back to your home. But I won't because, wóohitike. We'll call this counting first coup.

(Wóohitike tosses Marcus pretty far, then turns to Todd, who is already trying to run.)

Not so fast rez neck.

(Wóohitike grabs Todd and bends him into a pretzel or at least something uncomfortable.)

Gonna call this coup number two and not snap you in half. Deal?

(Todd is too terrified to move.)

I said, deal?
TODD: Yes. Coup sounds great.
WÓOHITIKE: And you will never bother these people again, correct?
TODD: I won't.
WÓOHITIKE: Then you are free to scurry.

(Wóohitike lets Todd go.)

ÁYA: Wait. I want an apology.
WÓOHITIKE: Nice touch.
TODD: I'm sorry?
ÁYA: For what?
TODD: Ummm...
ÁYA: You don't lay your hands on a person uninvited. Ever.
TODD: I'm sorry I touched you without asking.
ÁYA: It's called consent.
TODD: OK.
WÓOHITIKE: Scurry rez neck. Flee. And while you are at it, get off this reservation. We don't need you bottom feeders here.
TODD: But I have a right to—
WÓOHITIKE: Snap!

(Todd decides it's not worth it and scurries.)

ÁYA: Wow! That was incredible! Amazing! You literally threw Marcus. What else can you do?
WÓOHITIKE: I can move really big boulders. I mean if they want to be lifted. You know some Inyan want legs and some just wanna sit.
ÁYA: It's like the old stories. They really are true!

WÓOHITIKE: Of course they are.

ÁYA: I knew it! Could you crush a bike?

WÓOHITIKE: Yeah, sure.

ÁYA: Because there's this jerk from school who calls me the Girl-Boy so everyone laughs at me. He's got this bike that he LOVES. But he lives like ten miles out of town so we'd have to fly or teleport or whatever to get there.

WÓOHITIKE: I don't fly. I'm super strong. I thought that was obvious.

ÁYA: That's it? Super strength?

WÓOHITIKE: Well yeah. But it's pretty effective. I mean those two are . . . whoosh . . . gone. Not coming back.

ÁYA: But like right now, you can't really do anything useful for us?

WÓOHITIKE: I could throw you home. That's sort of like flying.

ÁYA: Then how do you get there?

WÓOHITIKE: I'd walk. Or run. I'm not slow. I do my cardio. But it's been hot, so not as much lately. It's more of a jog.

ÁYA: But how did you get here? You just appeared.

WÓOHITIKE: You brought me.

ÁYA: Me? I don't even know you.

WÓOHITIKE: I'm Wóohitike.

ÁYA: I got that. But I didn't know you existed, so how could I summon you?

WÓOHITIKE: I'm Wóohitike.

ÁYA: You gotta stop saying that.

WÓOHITIKE: But I am wóohitike. Like both with a big W and a little w. You used your wóohitike to bring me here.

ÁYA: Isn't that like bravery?

WÓOHITIKE: English is so limiting. That's how people translate it, I guess, but it is so much more. Your "bravery" brought me here. I am your bravery personified.

ÁYA: I wasn't brave. I was terrified. For Khoskalaka. The kids. Me.

WÓOHITIKE: But you used your super strength to protect the ones they wanted to hurt. Wóohitike.

ÁYA: Seriously, you can stop saying that. I mean, yeah, I led them away from our house. That was a little brave.

WÓOHITIKE: You were very brave and you did it without anyone getting hurt. Like with that knife you carry in your pocket. That is the bravest, to touch your enemy without harming them.

I bruised them a little, but you did it all without harm. That's super strength. That's—
ÁYA: Wóohitike.
WÓOHITIKE: Yes!
ÁYA: OK. So I . . . summoned you. Are you here to stay?
WÓOHITIKE: Am I?
ÁYA: Are you?
WÓOHITIKE: Am I?
ÁYA: Stop that. So . . . now what?
WÓOHITIKE: What what?
ÁYA: What happens?
WÓOHITIKE: Happens when?
ÁYA: Now.
WÓOHITIKE: Whatever you say.
ÁYA: Never mind.

(Áya is at a loss.)

I think you should come home and meet my brother. This is his area of expertise.
WÓOHITIKE: Great. Wanna jog?
ÁYA: No. We can just walk.

(They walk together back home.)

SCENE 7

Chorus Transition—Change

Again, this section can be done many ways with variations of movement and language and speakers.

CHORUS:
Things I want to change:
Taku bluthokča wachin:

The way we communicate.

The world.

My own attitude.

How I am seen.

Gangs.
ȟlete igluwita pi.

Abandoned houses.
Ti ahopha pi šni.

The safety of LGBTQ youth.

The people.

The way I respond to others.

The closeness of my family.

Being followed inside stores.
Masopiye wichihakab un pi.

Suicide.
Ič'ikte pi.

Blood quantum rights.

The way we live.

The way my people live.

The respect that elders get.

Lateral oppression.
Atayela wichakipažin pi.

Pressure to be perfect.
Wašte pi kta šilya wichapatinta pi.

Rape.
Šil owichakiȟ'an pi.

Haunted houses.
Tipi wanaǧi apawi pi.

The heat.

Dumb-ass wasicu people.
Wašiču takuni slolya pi šni.

Gunshots.
Maza wakhan kute pi.

Colorism.
Thoka wichakipažin pi.

Having to go to a massacre site to sell stuff to make money to live.
Okicize oyanke el ni pi kta un wawiyopheya pi.

Northside life.
Othunwahe waziya tanhan wicho'un.

Drugs.
Phežuta šiča.

Having to be good at sports.
Škata pi iyotan wachala chin pi.

Bullying.
Šilwachin pi.

Culture police.
Wicho'unye wichapasi pi.

Language police.
Wicho'iye wichakipažin pi.

Being kicked out of houses.
Tipi etan kathanka iyewichaya pi.

Murder.
Tiwichakte pi.

Kids taken from our people.
Waḱanyeža wichaki pi.

The threat of taking our kids.
Waḱanyeža unki pi kta wo'inapheke.

Racism.
Oyate anawichapta pi.

Racism.
Oyate anawichapta pi.

Racism.
Oyate anawichapta pi.

SCENE 8

Khoskalaka and Áya's Home—Morning

Wóohitike and Khoskalaka both sleep in the main room. Khoskalaka is surrounded by his schoolwork. He wakes, sees Wóohitike, and SCREAMS!

KHOSKALAKA: AAHHHHH!!

(Wóohitike jumps up, searching for the danger.)

WÓOHITIKE: What? Danger! I've got you!

(Áya rushes into the room as Khoskalaka raises his book as a weapon against Wóohitike.)

ÁYA: Stop! It's OK.
KHOSKALAKA: Who is that?
ÁYA: It's Wóohitike. You were asleep when we got in. I didn't want to wake you.

KHOSKALAKA: Wo-o-what?
ÁYA: Oh come on. Wóohitike. Bravery. That's her.
KHOSKALAKA: OK.
ÁYA: I mean you're the one always complaining that people don't know the language. Here's a pretty well-known word and—
KHOSKALAKA: I was distracted by the strange person you left sleeping next to me.
ÁYA: She's cool. She got rid of Todd.
KHOSKALAKA: How? That lurker has been hanging around for months now.
ÁYA: He was coming to hang on me.
KHOSKALAKA: Ew.
ÁYA: And you.
KHOSKALAKA: Ewwww. Why us?
ÁYA: The point is Wóohitike got rid of him. For good.

(Khoskalaka considers Wóohitike.)

KHOSKALAKA: Interesting outfit.
WÓOHITIKE: Thank you.
KHOSKALAKA: So you woke up one day and said, "This is my new look."
WÓOHITIKE: This is my only look.
KHOSKALAKA: You chose that? As a grown human?
WÓOHITIKE: No. This is how I appeared.
KHOSKALAKA: Appeared?
ÁYA: That's where you come in, Khoskalaka. We need your superhero expertise.
KHOSKALAKA: Superhero?
WÓOHITIKE: Áya summoned me.
KHOSKALAKA: You summoned her? How do you know her?
ÁYA: That's the thing, I don't. I was in trouble and was trying to be brave and she showed up and did some wild superhero action on Todd and Marcus while that Taté ran.
KHOSKALAKA: What kind of action?
ÁYA: Show him.

(Wóohitike performs a feat of amazing strength.)

KHOSKALAKA: Whoa. OK. Have you tried to un-summon her?

(Áya focuses on Wóohitike and tries really hard.)

ÁYA: Go. Be gone. I un-summon you. G-wan.

(She just stares back at them.)

Can't do it.

KHOSKALAKA: Great, another human to take care of.

ÁYA: Come on, it proves the old stories are true. What do you know about summoning superheroes?

KHOSKALAKA: A lot of times these things are triggered by an emotional point in your life. A time when you are at a crossroads. When you have a huge choice to make. What's the biggest choice you've ever had to make?

ÁYA: You know what it is. Last year when those bullies beat me up and we got in that fight and I left and went home and everything happened there and I was going to . . . you know.

(Kid One enters.)

KID ONE: Is it time for Cheerios?

KHOSKALAKA: Oh my gosh. We overslept. It's nearly time for the bus!

ÁYA: Everybody out for school! We're late!

(All of the kids run through. It's a scramble.)

ALL *(Ad-libbed)*: Where's my shoe? Don't forget your schoolwork. Take the Cheerio box and share on the way to the bus stop. Someone comb his hair! *(Etc.)*

(One of the older kids grabs the Cheerio box and doles out handfuls as they go.)

KHOSKALAKA: Listen to your teachers. Make good choices.
ÁYA: Eat your fruit at lunch.
WÓOHITIKE: Be brave!

(The kids stop at stare at Wóohitike.)

KID TWO: Who are you?
WÓOHITIKE: Wóohitike!
ÁYA: Say bye to Tunwin.
KID TWO: That's not my Tunwin.
ÁYA: Don't be disrespectful. Go! You're late!

> *(A kid pulls the door open. We hear a fearful growling and barking. They slam the door shut!)*

KID ONE: It's Hunter!

> *(The kids all SCREAM!)*

WÓOHITIKE: What kind of villain hunts children?
ÁYA: He's a really mean rez dog. We've all been bitten by Hunter.
KHOSKALAKA: Me, twice.
WÓOHITIKE: I will crush the evil sunka.

> *(Kid Two jumps in front of Wóohitike.)*

KID TWO: No! Don't hurt the puppy!

> *(Wóohitike isn't sure what to do. Áya is determined and gets a hot dog to lure Hunter away.*
> *Suddenly Wówačhiŋtȟaŋke appears in a superhero costume but also as an animal of some kind.)*

WÓOHITIKE: Hey, Wówačhiŋtȟaŋke.
WÓWAČHIŊTȞANKE: What's up, Wóohitike?
ÁYA: I totally understood him. I can talk to animals!
KHOSKALAKA: He's speaking English.
ÁYA: Oh.
KHOSKALAKA: But that is pretty cool.
ÁYA: It's another superhero.

> *(Hunter snarls and jumps at the door. Everyone SCREAMS.)*

WÓWAČHIŊTȞANKE: Who's the villain?
WÓOHITIKE: Child-eating Hunter that must be gotten rid of but not harmed.

WÓWAČHIŊTȞAŊKE: I'm on it.

(*Wówačhiŋtȟaŋke changes into a bird. He flies out the window and lands behind Hunter. He changes into a bear and growls. Hunter yelps and runs away. Wówačhiŋtȟaŋke returns as a huge bear.*)

ALL: Whoa!
KHOSKALAKA: Who are you?
WÓWAČHIŊTȞAŊKE: I am Wówačhiŋtȟaŋke.
KHOSKALAKA: Perseverance. I know that one. It's perseverance.
ÁYA: You get an A.

(*We hear a bus horn.*)

KHOSKALAKA: The bus!

(*The kids run out. Kid Two gives Wówačhiŋtȟaŋke a hug.*)

KID TWO: Wopila Leksi.
WÓWAČHIŊTȞAŊKE: Toksá.
KHOSKALAKA: Go!

(*They do.*)

WÓWAČHIŊTȞAŊKE: What's the plan now?
WÓOHITIKE: Not sure. It must be big if we were both summoned.
ÁYA: No one was summoned. We were trying to figure out why the first one was here, and then a new one showed up.
KHOSKALAKA: Can you be any animal you want?
WÓWAČHIŊTȞAŊKE: I can now.
KHOSKALAKA: Do you have an origin story?
WÓWAČHIŊTȞAŊKE: Of course.
KHOSKALAKA: I loooove origin stories.
ÁYA: Or as non-nerds call them, "stories."
KHOSKALAKA: Shhh!
WÓWAČHIŊTȞAŊKE: Then I will tell you my origin story of how I learned to control my power.
KHOSKALAKA: Yes!

SCENE 9

Wówačhiŋthaŋke's Story—Taku Wašte Kte

We enter Wówačhiŋthaŋke's story as it is acted out in front of us. In the original production, it was told entirely in Lakota with a puppet theater acting it out next to the speaker.
    Bullies hassle Wówačhiŋthaŋke, teasing him and pushing him around.

WÓWAČHIŊTȞANKE: Wamakhanyeža hehan mathokeča. Wamakhanškan mataku kte ki yuswa'un owakihi šni. Oyate yuš'inwichawaye, mititakuye koya. Mithankš ti ekta wa'un kta un iyayewakiye, tomakeča keyaš temaȟila wan he. Tuwa tanyan awichayanka pi chin pi hantaš tiwahe wan tuwe keyaš thawa pi wan he unkiye pi.
    [As a child, I was different. I could not control what kind of animal I was. It scared people, even my own family. I ran away to live with my sister, the one who loved me no matter what form I took. We became a family to everyone who needed a place to be safe.]

Hekta omakha wanži oyate šiča el mahi pi. Makipažin pi na amayuštan pi šni. Echin mataku ki okaȟniǧa pi šni. Tokeške namič'ižin kte ki unmaspe šni. Ksuye maya pi. [A year ago, I was faced with evil villains. They hounded me and would not leave me alone because they did not understand what I was. I did not know how to defend myself. They hurt me.]

(Wówačhiŋtȟaŋke is a small rabbit, and the bullies hurt him.)

Michante ki a'iyokpasye pi. Temaȟila ȟča ki taku tokha ki imayuǧan pi kta han hoka mahingnin na wichawakuwa. Hechena imayuthan pi ečan mnaža mahingni na womakhokpe na ochin-mašiča cha naphewichawaye.
[My heart was darkened by it. When my most beloved one tried to talk to me about what happened, I became a badger and turned on them. They kept trying until I turned into a mountain lion and was so fierce and mean that I scared them away.]

(A person tries to care for Wówačhiŋtȟaŋke, but he pushes them away. They keep trying and keep getting pushed away. Finally Wówačhiŋtȟaŋke "wins" and hurts the other person enough that they stop trying.)

Watohanya michunkši oyazanwaye ki wanblaka cha iwakiye. Ayes ehani wati hechi waki hel taku šiče ȟča wan wamakhaskan mačikala hehan makize. Hektakiya wichawakiza owakihi šni na makiza pi ohakab ithunkala čik'ala mahingle.
[I could see how much I had hurt my sister, so I ran away. But I went back to my old home, where the worst villain of all attacked me when I was just a small creature. I was not able to fight them off, and after the attack, I became a little mouse.]

(Through the following, Wówačhiŋtȟaŋke becomes a tiny flea.)

He ohakab, lila čik'ala mič'ichaǧe hechel matakuni kte šni cha lila kiyela iwanblakin na psičala mič'ichaǧe. O'ali el tuwa aphe manke hechel u na namat'in kte. Ayeš hehan mitha tewichawaȟila wichaweksuye na čikčikala ki awawichunglaka pi hena.

[After that, I wanted to make myself so small that I would cease to exist, so I focused as hard as I could and turned myself into a flea. I sat on the stair, waiting for someone to come along and crush me. But then I thought of my beloved one and the little ones we cared for together.]
 Taku ota ehani blusni hena awiblukcan na tokhamah'an ki iyoksiča pi kta cha slolwaye. Mikpanažin owakihi cha slolwaye na wa'awakipha he thokatakiya imakaǧi wakiyin kte šni. Matanyan kta cha slolwaye. Cha ake iwanblakin na thaȟča mič'ičaǧe na oyanke šiča hetan thehan iyayewakiye,wati ȟča heči.
 [I thought of all that I had overcome already and knew that if I disappeared, I would be missed. I knew that I had resilience, and that I would not let my trauma define my future. I knew that it was going to be OK. So I focused again and made myself into a deer and ran far from that bad place, back to my real home.]

(Wówačhiŋthaŋke becomes a deer.)

Hehantan migluthokeča owakihi wamakha thokthokča wachin hantanaš. Ca, takun yachin hantanaš el chichi'un pi kte yelo.
 [Ever since then I have been able to change into different animals at will. So, whatever you need, I am at your service.]

SCENE 10

Khoskalaka and Áya's Home—Continuous

We return to the present. Áya is stunned. Wówačhiŋthaŋke occasionally changes to different animals.

KHOSKALAKA: Áya, that's *your* story.

ÁYA: I know.

KHOSKALAKA: It's literally what happened to you last year. Wówa-čhiŋthaŋke, how is it that your origin story is Áya's story?

WÓWAČHIŊTȞANKE: That is a good question.

KHOSKALAKA: That's it? Any more clues?

WÓWAČHIŊTȞANKE: To what?

KHOSKALAKA: To why you are telling Áya's story as your origin story?

WÓWAČHIŊTȞANKE: I don't know, but if you say that's what is true, I believe you. You are the most beloved of Áya, so you would not lie.

KHOSKALAKA: That still doesn't explain why you two are here, and that's concerning. Look, I like comic books and superhero movies, but we need a real expert. We need to go to Rapid.

ÁYA: Why there?
KHOSKALAKA: Because the biggest Native superhero nerd I know works at a comic book store in Rapid. If anyone can figure this out, he can.
ÁYA: Oh! The Blow Up the Faces Rally!
KHOSKALAKA: No rally. And I meant this weekend, after these two go . . . home?
WÓOHITIKE: We will not leave you in a time of crisis.
ÁYA: Come on, Khoskalaka, if we don't go now, I bet they will keep multiplying.
KHOSKALAKA: I need to study for my test.
ÁYA: I'll drive and you can study on the road.
KHOSKALAKA: But—
ÁYA: Brother, two superheroes literally materialized in front of us and you are worried about a test?
KHOSKALAKA: But—
WÓWAČHIŊTȞAŊKE: Khoskalaka, when Wóohitike and I are summoned, it is for a reason. An important, immediate reason. If we can determine the reason before it finds us, we have an advantage beyond strength and form.
KHOSKALAKA: Right. You're right. This is like my ultimate fantasy. I fear something big is going down.

(Wóohitike takes an alert stance, ready for danger. Wówačhiŋtȟaŋke turns into a rattlesnake, ready to strike.)

WÓOHITIKE: I knew it!
WÓWAČHIŊTȞAŊKE: We will vanquish the evil—
KHOSKALAKA: Calm down. There isn't a threat at this moment. Let me grab my books and call the school so it's an excused absence. I'll tell them I have a doctor's appointment in Rapid.
ÁYA. Yes!
KHOSKALAKA: We are getting help, then coming straight back. No rally!

(As Khoskalaka gets his stuff together, Áya considers Wówačhiŋtȟaŋke and Wóohitike.)

ÁYA: I have enough issues with people noticing me in a bad way. I need you two to take it down a notch. Some people off the rez aren't very accepting when it comes to Native folks like us and people dressed like . . . you.

(Wówačhiŋthaŋke changes form.)

And that can't happen on the street. We all gotta code switch at times. Be something normal. Like a dog.

(He changes into a fluffy poodle.)

WÓWAČHIŊTȞANKE: Woof.
ÁYA: A rez dog.

(He changes into a big rez dog.)

WÓWAČHIŊTȞANKE: Woof. Aye.
ÁYA: This isn't going to go well. I can tell already.

SCENE II

Chorus Transition—Superpower

A dance of movement, of travel, of covering space and time. Of passing local places. Of seeing beautiful scenery. A road trip. All while Khoskalaka tries to study.

CHORUS:
    My superpower is:
    Mitha wowaš'ake hča ki:

    Complimenting people. It's the best smile.
    Oyate wichayu'onihan. Iha pi ki wašte hča.

    Sleeping.
    Ištima pi.

    Making people mad.
    Oyate wichayuchanzeka.

Basketball.
Thapa.

Silly jokes.
Owehanhan woyake.

Getting up no matter how hard I fall.
Ičat'a wagliȟpaye ayeš nažin wahiyaye.

Sitting quietly for three hours.
O'aphe yamni inila yanke.

Making people happy, even when I'm at my worst.
Emachetu ke šni ayeš, hechena oyate i'okipi wicawaye.

Speaking my language.
Mita wicho'iye weč'un.

My intelligence.
Mitha woslolye.

Recognizing and processing my emotions.
Mitha wo'achin ki iyewakinying n aapiwakiye.

Naming countries. I can do a lot.
Makhoče chašwathun. Taku ota owakihi.

I can see what's behind the language people use.
Oyate wicho'iye tokel un pi ki wanblaka owakihi.

Writing poetry.
Wichoyake owa pi.

Talking.
Iya pi. Lila iwaya owakihi.

I can comfort people when they are sad.
Oyate i'okšiča pi hantanaš ahanzil wichawaya owakihi.

Comedy.
Owehanhan ikpazo pi.

My family.
Mititakuye.

My superpower is my ability to keep moving.
Mitha wošʼake hča ki un thokatakiya ya wablupike.

My superpower is my essence. Me.
Mitha wošʼake ki mitawachin, Miye.

My superpower is giving to others.
Mitha wowašʼske un wawichawakʼu.

My superpower is being a caretaker.
Mitha wowašʼake ki un waʼawanblake.

Being Dakhota.
Dakota hecha.

Being Lakhota.
Lakota hecha.

Being Nakhota.
Nakota hecha.

SCENE 12

Driving in Rapid City

Áya drives with Khoskalaka next to them and the superheroes in the back.
   Khoskalaka unfolds a paper map. Like in the days of paper maps, he's struggling with it. It's folding up on him and generally not going well.

ÁYA: Welcome to Rapid City. Have you two been here?
WÓWAČHIŊTȞANKE: We are all from here. It is the heart of everything that is.
ÁYA: Sure. I meant the town.
WÓOHITIKE: I don't know.
ÁYA: Great. Hey, Khoskalaka, do I turn or not? I gotta change lanes if we're not turning.
KHOSKALAKA: I'm trying!
ÁYA: Khoskalaka! We missed the turn.

   (Khoskalaka studies the map.)

KHOSKALAKA: We must be here, so . . . that wasn't it.
ÁYA: You have got to use your phone like a normal person. We actually have tons of signal for once.
KHOSKALAKA: Do you have any idea how much data navigation apps use? I need my data for school research. If a paper map was good enough for our ancestors, it's good enough for us.
WÓOHITIKE: I've never seen an ancestor with a paper map.
ÁYA: When do I turn, Lala?
KHOSKALAKA: We've got . . . two more blocks.
ÁYA: Oh no.
KHOSKALAKA: Oh yes. Well, one now.
ÁYA: No, we're being pulled over.
KHOSKALAKA: Oh crap. Stupid Rapid.
ÁYA: We just got here and we're already getting a DWN.
WÓWAČHIŊTȞANKE: What's that?
KHOSKALAKA: Driving While Native.

(Áya pulls over and a police officer approaches the car.)

OFFICER *(Overly friendly)*: Hey there little . . . lady? License, insurance, and registration. How are you doing?

(Áya slowly and carefully gets her license out while Khoskalaka hands over the other documents.)

ÁYA: I was doing better before I got pulled over.
KHOSKALAKA: What's the problem, Officer?
OFFICER: You folks live around here?
KHOSKALAKA: No. We're just in town for the day.
OFFICER: Yeah, saw the tribal plates.
ÁYA: I bet you did.
OFFICER: What you say?
ÁYA: Nothing. Do I have a turn signal out or something?
OFFICER: Why don't you turn off the car and I'll do a little looking into these papers? Sound good?
KHOSKALAKA: Yes. Thank you.

(The officer goes.)

ÁYA: Thank you?
KHOSKALAKA: I bet you did?
WÓOHITIKE: Shall I crush him if he comes back?
WÓWAČHIŊTȞAŊKE: I could become a bison and double crush him.
KHOSKALAKA: No. We'll let you know if we need you.
WÓWAČHIŊTȞAŊKE: Do you agree, Áya?
ÁYA: Yeah. Just chill.

(They do. The officer returns and hands the papers and license back.)

OFFICER: You aren't going to that rally are you?
ÁYA: The Blow Up—
KHOSKALAKA: No.
ÁYA: No.
OFFICER: Because I'd have to report you for truancy if that's what you're doing.
KHOSKALAKA: I have a doctor's appointment. It's an excused absence. You can call the school.
OFFICER: Lots of folks heading down to the faces. There's gonna be some trouble there.

(He looks in the back seat.)

And what about you? You having a good day?
WÓOHITIKE: Yes.
OFFICER: That's a big dog.
WÓWAČHIŊTȞAŊKE: Woof.
OFFICER *(To Wóohitike)*: You have any drugs on you?
WÓOHITIKE: No.
OFFICER: Not even "sacred" ones? Because that may fly on the reservation but it's illegal here.
KHOSKALAKA: We don't do drugs.
OFFICER: Not hiding any in that bundle of sage are you? Because that won't fool the drug dogs.
KHOSKALAKA: It's just sage.

(The officer reaches in and takes the sage bundle. Áya flinches but manages to resist grabbing it back.

The officer pulls out a knife, cuts the string, and breaks the sage apart, searching through it. He hands the torn-up bits of sage back to Áya.)

OFFICER: Yep. Looks OK. Well, you kids have a good doctor's visit and safe drive back home.
KHOSKALAKA: As soon as we can.
OFFICER: OK then. Enjoy.

(He goes.)

WÓWAČHIŊTȞANKE: Why are we letting the villain go free?
ÁYA: Because there is something bigger for us to do. I can feel it.
WÓWAČHIŊTȞANKE: Wise to save our strength for the true fight.
ÁYA: Yeah. Hope so.
KHOSKALAKA: Turn left at the end of the block and it's right there.

(They drive to the comic shop parking lot.)

SCENE 13

Comic Store Parking Lot—Rapid City

KHOSKALAKA: I think I should go in first. Don't want to overwhelm him or draw too much nerd attention.
WÓOHITIKE: Do you think they have a bathroom?
KHOSKALAKA: For what?
WÓOHITIKE: You want a number?
KHOSKALAKA: You can't hold it?
WÓOHITIKE: I really gotta go.
KHOSKALAKA: Fine, but try to look less . . . you.

(They go, leaving the other two in the car.)

WÓWAČHIŊTȞANKE: Why do you have issues with people noticing you in a bad way?
ÁYA: You really listen.
WÓWAČHIŊTȞANKE: I have an excellent memory.
ÁYA: It's my gender identity.

WÓWAČHIŊTȞAŊKE: What is?

ÁYA: The reason I have problems.

WÓWAČHIŊTȞAŊKE: What is your gender identity?

ÁYA: I'm not sure. I just always have felt . . . wrong as a girl. I don't hate being a girl, but it's like people think I'm one thing on the outside, but inside I feel different. Like I don't know how to fit in my own skin.

WÓWAČHIŊTȞAŊKE: I know that feeling! I don't remember which me is the true me anymore. I feel like I was something else once, but I can't get back to it for some reason.

ÁYA: I'm sorry. I still dress more like a girl because it's safer. But I know this isn't me. Or not all of me.

WÓWAČHIŊTȞAŊKE: You are lucky to know which you is the real you.

ÁYA: Not really. The real me is . . . a problem. It's a lot different from this.

WÓWAČHIŊTȞAŊKE: I hope to find the real me again one day.

ÁYA: When you do, will you stop changing forms?

WÓWAČHIŊTȞAŊKE: I'll still change, but I'll have a strong foundation to return to. Imagine, if I have this much power now, how much more power I will have when I know the true me?

ÁYA: Maybe it works that way wherever you are from, but here it's different. Being the real me makes makes me a target, not powerful.

(The others return with a super enthusiastic Chris, the Native nerd. Chris is an elder. He rushes to the car and looks in.)

CHRIS: I love it. You're both totally different, yet there's something in the same vein you know? Like you're from the same universe and timeline.

ÁYA: They know each other.

CHRIS: Awesome! Show me the stuff.

ÁYA: Wait, this is the superhero expert?

KHOSKALAKA: Yeah, this is Chris.

ÁYA: He's . . . not . . . like us.

KHOSKALAKA: Yeah, he's Dakota but I don't hold it against him.

CHRIS: Ayee!

KHOSKALAKA: I didn't know you're such a D snob.

ÁYA: No, he's ol . . . an eld . . . not what I expected.

CHRIS: You think your generation invented superheroes? Kit Walker, a.k.a. The Phantom, debuted in 1936. Superman dates back to 1938. And don't get me started on cultural figures with superpowers, those go back to the beginning of time.
ÁYA: OK. You're clearly the expert.
CHRIS: So, show me the stuff.
ÁYA: What stuff?
CHRIS: The powers. I gotta see them!
ÁYA: No. Not here.
CHRIS: Please, no one has come in all day. It will help me figure out what's happening.
ÁYA: Fine. But quickly.
CHRIS *(To Wóohitike)*: Can you lift the whole car? With them in it?
WÓOHITIKE: Easy.

(She approaches the car.)

ÁYA: No lifting cars! What if someone comes and she's got a car over her head? Something smaller. Easier to hide.
WÓOHITIKE: I could just lift one end. Like this.

(Wóohitike lifts one side of the car, tilting Wówačhiŋtȟaŋke and Áya inside.)

CHRIS: Wopida! Khoskalaka, this is incredible!
ÁYA: OK, that's enough, put us down.
CHRIS *(To Wówačhiŋtȟaŋke)*: Now you.

(Wówačhiŋtȟaŋke looks to Áya.)

ÁYA: Go for it.

(Wówačhiŋtȟaŋke gets out of the car and is suddenly a different form.)

CHRIS: Pinch me. For real, right on my arm. *(To Áya)* And they are both connected to Áya?
WÓWAČHIŊTȞANKE: Of course.

CHRIS: He talks! You all heard him talk, right?
KHOSKALAKA: Yes, the animal talks.
ÁYA: They keep saying I summoned them.
CHRIS: So we gotta figure out why.
ÁYA: No kidding.
CHRIS: But what's your quest?
WÓWAČHIŊTȞAŊKE: Yet to be determined.
KHOSKALAKA: That seems to be the extent of their knowledge of what is happening here.
CHRIS: But you two know each other?
WÓOHITIKE: Of course.
CHRIS: But from where? Did you fight a super villain together? Were you summoned elsewhere?
WÓOHITIKE: We have always known each other. Like the oyate have always known us. We are parts of the same thing.
CHRIS: Not very specific, are they?
WÓOHITIKE: I thought I was exceptionally clear.
WÓWAČHIŊTȞAŊKE: I understood you.
WÓOHITIKE: Thanks, Wówačhiŋtȟaŋke.
CHRIS: OK. So the key is Áya. What are your biggest enemies?
ÁYA: Um, the same as everyone. Racism. Poverty. Drugs. Capitalism. Colonial societal structures. Destruction of the environment. Land Back. Humidity.

(Chris thinks.)

CHRIS: But you ended up here. Nothing on a quest happens by chance. You are in Rapid for a reason.
ÁYA: Yeah, you.
CHRIS: No, this place is specific. There is a conflict, a battle, you need to wage here.
KHOSKALAKA: A battle? Wait, we gotta be back when the youth center bus drops the kids off at five.
ÁYA: We might not make it back by then, Khoskalaka. We can get someone to stay with them tonight.
KHOSKALAKA: I can't stay the night. We have school tomorrow.
ÁYA: Stop with school! This is real life, a real quest.
KHOSKALAKA: But my test is tomorrow. I can't miss it.

ÁYA: Look, I've got nothing in my future but trying not to screw up those kids. I have a feeling in my gut that this is my thing. Like this is the real crossroads of my life and I've gotta go for it with all I've got.

KHOSKALAKA: Fine, but I know in my gut that I need to get back to school.

ÁYA: Oh my god. We do literally everything you want. Let me have one thing.

KHOSKALAKA: Are you kidding me?

ÁYA: No. Not at all.

KHOSKALAKA: I am giving up everything for you. To stay with you. To help you.

ÁYA: For one stupid day.

KHOSKALAKA: For four years. I'm giving up my ultimate dream for four years.

ÁYA: What are you talking about?

(Khoskalaka pulls the letter out of his pocket. Áya reads quickly while the others read over her shoulder.)

CHRIS: A full ride! That's incredible. Congratulations!

(They cheer happily.)

WÓOHITIKE: Wóohitike!

WÓWAČHIŊTȞAŊKE: Wówačhiŋtȟaŋke!

ÁYA: Wait. *(To Khoskalaka)* You are leaving us for four years?

KHOSKALAKA: I'm not going. That's the point.

ÁYA: But you applied. They didn't just find your name online and say, "Hey let's offer that poor Lakota guy in the middle of nowhere a scholarship." You applied.

KHOSKALAKA: Yeah. I did. To lots of places. This is my dream.

ÁYA: Fine. Then go.

KHOSKALAKA: Maybe I will.

CHRIS: You have to, Khoskalaka.

ÁYA: Leave us. We don't need you.

KHOSKALAKA: Are you kidding me? You can't match two socks without me.

ÁYA: I like my socks mismatched. Just leave!
KHOSKALAKA: Fine. Then I'm gone.
ÁYA: I can't wait to sleep without your snoring.
KHOSKALAKA: Well you'll have four years of great sleep.
ÁYA: Go right now.
KHOSKALAKA: What?
ÁYA: You have your own dream. Go follow it.
KHOSKALAKA: It's next school year.
ÁYA: I don't want you here.
KHOSKALAKA: We came in one car.
ÁYA: Go away! This is my quest and you're ruining it!
KHOSKALAKA: You can't be—
ÁYA: Get out!!

(Áya gestures at Khoskalaka and they fly backward against the car. Whoa.)

KHOSKALAKA: What did you—
ÁYA: I'm warning you. Leave. Now.

(Áya makes a threatening gesture like they are going to do the same thing again.
  Khoskalaka gets in the car.)

KHOSKALAKA: You do this every time. When things get hard you push everyone who loves you away.
ÁYA: You left first.

(Khoskalaka drives away. Áya turns to the remaining crew.)

What just happened?
CHRIS: Well, you lost your brother and were really petty about it.
ÁYA: No. The energy or whatever. What was that?
CHRIS: I'm guessing it's part of your quest. Can you do it again?

(Áya turns to try on a rock. Everyone else ducks behind each other. Áya tries hard. Nothing happens.)

WÓOHITIKE: That's unfortunate.

WÓWAČHIŊTȞAŊKE: You need to learn the key to your power.
CHRIS: Maybe it is anger?
ÁYA: Doesn't that make me a villain?
CHRIS: Everyone has the potential to be a hero or a villain. It's all in how you choose to use your powers.
ÁYA: Well, I don't have any power right now. So . . . do you have a car we can use?
CHRIS: Nope. Where are we going?
WÓOHITIKE: To find the villain.
WÓWAČHIŊTȞAŊKE: And the big battle.
CHRIS: Well, hopefully the villain and battle are on a bus route, because I take the bus.

(They think. A small bus pulls into the parking lot. A Native person drives.)

NATIVE PERSON: Hey, do you know how to get to Mount Rushmore? I'm trying to get to the Blow Up the Faces Rally.
ÁYA: That's it! You said I'm in Rapid for a reason, right?
CHRIS: Yeah, that is how it works. Your destiny finds you and becomes undeniable.
ÁYA: I've wanted to go to this rally since I heard of it. Then we had to come here to find you. The officer told us there would be trouble there. That's gotta be *our* trouble! Now Khoskalaka is gone and a bus appears to take us there.
WÓOHITIKE: Let's go.
WÓWAČHIŊTȞAŊKE: Shotgun.

(They run for the bus.)

NATIVE PERSON: You may not want to arrive with me. I'm supposed to order food for a feed, but I lost my wallet and can't pay for it. I'm gonna have to tell a lot of hungry Indians that there's nothing to eat.
ÁYA: Does anyone have money?
CHRIS: I've got a senior bus pass.

(Áya pulls a necklace from under their shirt.)

ÁYA: My unci's necklace. It's real gold.

(Wóohitike and Wówachiŋtȟaŋke exchange a look.)

WÓOHITIKE: That would be very generous.
WÓWACHIŊTȞANKE: An important act of giving.
ÁYA: Cool. Let's pawn this and order food before we leave town.
CHRIS: Are you sure you don't want to go after Khoskalaka?
ÁYA: If you feel some kind of way about it because he's your friend, then go. We have a battle to get to.

(Chris is torn. But he looks to Wówachiŋtȟaŋke and Wóohitike.)

CHRIS: I know a guy who will give you a fair price.

(They all go together.)

SCENE 14

Mount Rushmore—Blow Up the Faces Rally

Four presidents in stone loom over our group. On one side are folks chanting to blast the mountain. On the other side are counter protesters and confused tourists. They all yell at each other.
  We join our crew, scanning the crowd.

CHRIS: If we are looking for a fight, this is definitely the place.
WÓWAČHIŊTȞAŊKE: It is proof of Áya's destiny.
WÓOHITIKE: When you are on the right path, everything conspires to keep you moving forward.
ÁYA: So I'm not going to be a villain?
WÓWAČHIŊTȞAŊKE: That is yet to be seen.
WÓOHITIKE: This all could be moving you forward to your destruction.
CHRIS: Or the destruction of the planet.
ÁYA: Great. Now what do we do?
CHRIS: We wait for something to happen.

(They wait.)

BLOW UP THE FACES PERSON: Hey, where's the free food?
COUNTER PROTESTER: I'm hungry too.

(And just like, that the two sides unite in a chant for food. It turns dark really fast.)

WÓOHITIKE: This is making me nervous. Want me to shut them up?

(She flexes. A lot.)

WÓWAČHIŊTȞANKE: We did promise food to the Indians.
WÓOHITIKE: I could eat.
CHRIS: Rule one when gathering Indians: there must be food.
ÁYA: I know. I sold my jewelry for that food.

(They check their phone.)

Oh no! The delivery person has a flat. We should have waited for it.
CHRIS: We can go meet them.
ÁYA: They are just outside of Rapid. By the time we go there and back, this will be a riot. We need a better solution to feed these people.

(Wówačhaŋtognake appears. Her power is super speed.)

WÓWAČHAŊTOGNAKE: I've got this.
WÓOHITIKE: Wówačhaŋtognake! Perfect.
CHRIS: Generosity and compassion. Of course.
ÁYA: How can you help?

(Wówačhaŋtognake runs away and reappears absurdly fast with a bag of food.)

CHRIS: Wopida! That was fast.
WÓWAČHAŊTOGNAKE: I could go faster but I'm trying not to spill the food.

(She repeats this several times until all the food has been retrieved.)

ÁYA: That was amazing! Now we can—
WÓWAČHAŊTOGNAKE: Not done yet.

(She distributes the food super fast. In a moment it all disappears. Protesters suddenly have food in their hands. They eat.)

ÁYA: Wait. That food was for our people.

(Wówačhaŋtognake joins our group.)

WÓWAČHAŊTOGNAKE: That's not how wówačhaŋtognake works. What else do you have to give?
ÁYA: I don't have anything left.
WÓWAČHAŊTOGNAKE: You most certainly do.
ÁYA: Just my clothes and personal stuff.
WÓWAČHAŊTOGNAKE: Precisely. Tell me where that is and I will retrieve it.
ÁYA: You are going to get my stuff? Why?
WÓWAČHAŊTOGNAKE: To give away.
ÁYA: But we gave all of them food. And my jewelry.
WÓWAČHAŊTOGNAKE: What about your medicine bag?
ÁYA: I got it at my Isnati ceremony.
WÓWAČHAŊTOGNAKE: But the true giveaway is to give all. Hold nothing back.
ÁYA: I'm not giving all of my stuff to strangers. I need things. To live. And we can't just go buy more.
WÓWAČHAŊTOGNAKE: But wówačhaŋtognake means trust in being provided for.
ÁYA: That hasn't been my experience so far. In life.
CHRIS: That is the old way to do a giveaway. Today we go buy things, extra things to give. But in the old way you would give away everything you had. Like everything.
ÁYA: But these people should be giving things to me. It's our land.
WÓWAČHAŊTOGNAKE: That's not how wówačhaŋtognake works.
WÓWAČHIŊTȞANKE: That's true.
COUNTER PROTESTER: That was my drink!

BLOW UP THE FACES PERSON: I didn't get one.
COUNTER PROTESTER: Too bad.

(They grab the drink back.)

BLOW UP THE FACES PERSON: Not today, colonizer!

(It immediately turns into a scuffle. It's more comical than violent, but completely earnest. The violence spreads through the crowd instantly.)

WÓWAČHAŊTOGNAKE: Told you.
ÁYA: Giving these people my jeans with holes in them would not have stopped this.
WÓWAČHAŊTOGNAKE: It would have relieved the tension. Time to get to work, my friends. It's the moment they have been waiting for.

(Wówačhaŋtognake, Wówačhiŋthaŋke, and Wóohitike take their superhero stance. It's the Big Fight. Each of our heroes takes on someone from the crowd in a funny way: slow motion, fast, silly, all of it. During these battles, Chris tries to figure it out.)

CHRIS: Maybe the villain isn't one person but a way of being. This greed and fighting, it's not the Dakota way. Or Lakota.
WÓWAČHIŊTȞANKE: Or Nakota.
CHRIS: This crabs-in-the-bucket mentality. Tearing each other down. Treating each other different because of our race. Expecting someone to save us when we have the means to save ourselves.
WÓWAČHAŊTOGNAKE: We're trying. Our heroes aren't being defeated, but they aren't making progress.
CHRIS: So you were sent the virtues—bravery, perseverance, and generosity—to put things right. Still no progress. It's like Agent Smith, the fighting people never stop coming.
ÁYA: But it's not working.
CHRIS: Wisdom! There are four cardinal virtues. We are missing wisdom to make them complete. Áya, summon Wóksape. Now!

(Áya tries.)

ÁYA: Wisdom! Wóksape, I summon you. We need you now.
WÓOHITIKE: We really do.

(Nothing.)

CHRIS: Keep trying!
ÁYA: Come on, Wóksape! I command wisdom. I am thinking really smart things. Please? *(To Chris)* It's no use. Khoskalaka is the smart one. I depend on his brain.
CHRIS: That's it. Wówačhaŋtognake! We need Khoskalaka to complete this! He's on Highway 40 by now.
WÓWAČHAŊTOGNAKE: I will be back momentarily.

(She goes and returns instantly with Khoskalaka.)

KHOSKALAKA: What the—
ÁYA: I am sorry. I was selfish and wrong. I want you to go to college. I want you to follow your dreams. Go get all of the wisdom. We will be fine. Pretty wise of me, right?
KHOSKALAKA: I guess. I'm sorry too. I should have told you I was applying to schools.

(They hug. The angry people surround our superheroes and close in. It's looking bad.)

CHRIS: Where is Wóksape? We need them to complete the circle.
KHOSKALAKA: Wisdom? That's up to Áya. With the other ones, Áya showed the virtue themselves and the superhero appeared. Show wisdom, Áya.
ÁYA: That's what you are here for.
KHOSKALAKA: No. It has to be you. Wisdom is honesty. The old ways. It's harmony with all things.

(Our heroes are overtaken one by one by the crowd.)

ÁYA: I am harmonious. I accept all people as they are. Except stupid wasicus.
WÓWAČHAŊTOGNAKE: That's not very generous of you.

ÁYA: Fine, I can give them harmony too. And half of my food.
KHOSKALAKA: What about yourself?
ÁYA: I don't understand.
KHOSKALAKA: You aren't in harmony with yourself.
ÁYA: I'm trying.
KHOSKALAKA: Do or do not.
CHRIS AND KHOSKALAKA: There is no try!
CHRIS: Yes. Áya, you have to be in harmony with you. Then Wóksape will appear.
ÁYA: But people won't accept me that way.

(Our heroes are nearly gone.)

KHOSKALAKA: It's the old way. Be you. All of you. No more fighting with who you are.
CHRIS: Now!
ÁYA: I am . . .

(Áya makes a grand dramatic gesture to shed the female expression of themselves and transitions before our eyes to a trans man, with a little flair that holds their female power too. It's Clark Kent into Superman. Instant and awesome. We wonder why we didn't always see it. From here on, Áya is now Ahí. Ahí speaks entirely in Lakota.)

AHÍ: Ahí. Wani. [Ahí. I have become.]

(Khoskalaka and Chris look around for Wóksape.)

KHOSKALAKA: Where is Wóksape? It's almost too late! Our heroes are gone.
AHÍ: Woksape miye. Lel wa'un. [I am Wóksape. I am here.]

(Ahí reaches out to the crowd and does the mind-moving thing, but gently and carefully. Everyone is moved carefully away from our heroes. The people are puzzled but unable to resist.)

KHOSKALAKA: Your power!

NATIVE NATION PROJECT

CHRIS: You can control it now.

(Our heroes emerge and each takes a direction of the area. With Ahí they become the four directions. They look at the completed circle with pride. First, Wówačhaŋtognake acknowledges Ahí. Something happens. Ahí takes Wówačhaŋtognake's power. He does something super fast.)

WÓWAČHAŊTOGNAKE: Your generosity honors you.

(Wówačhaŋtognake goes. Wówačhiŋtȟaŋke does the same. Giving Ahí his power. Ahí turns into an animal. Wówačhiŋtȟaŋke turns into a human, their true form.)

WÓWAČHIŊTȞANKE: It's me. You've given me back myself.

(Wówačhiŋtȟaŋke goes as Ahí becomes human again. Finally, Wóohitike gleefully gives super strength to Ahí, who responds by lifting Wóohitike into the air and throwing them out of the area.)

WÓOHITIKE: I'm flying!
CHRIS: Ahí, it was all you. All of them were always you.
KHOSKALAKA: You just had to claim your power. Winyan and wichasa. It's you.
CHRIS: Now you have all of their powers as yours. And the mind-moving thing.
AHÍ: Akta yukhe. Itazipa na wahinkpe maka'u wo. [There's more. Bring me a bow and arrow.]

(Ahí performs a broadly incredible feat of shooting. Perhaps hitting two birds and a rabbit with one arrow.)

Šunka wakhan wan. [A horse.]

(Ahí performs an unbelievable feat of horsemanship.)

Nitha phehin ki. [Your hair.]

(Someone with long hair comes to Ahí. He instantly turns their flowing hair into perfect, tight braids. Ahí is super L/Dakota. Ahí turns into a wolf and has a conversation with another wolf, in Dakota.)

(In Dakota) Minsun, hanhepi unk'iyanke kte na nitha odowan kin nititakuye ob awahiyaye kte. [Brother, I will run with you tonight and sing your songs with your family.]

(Ahí and the wolf howl together.)

(In Lakota) Yunkhan he Dakota hecha. [That was Dakota, by the way.]

(The people watching are both awed and scared.)

Mitakuye pi. Wowayanke hena bluštan kta ča wahi hena thanka ki unkakičiyuštan pi. Wowaš'ake mithawa ki oyate ki iwašte pi kta ča weč'un kte. Oyate ki iyuha. Iyuha kapah̆ wowah̆wa na woyuha hektakiya unkaku pi kte. Unkiye iyuha wakhan wo'ečun ki el ungli pi kte. Išanti Awichalowanpi, Hanblečeyapi na uma ki iyuha. Iyuha kapah̆ taku thanila hena lečala kağaya unk'un pi kte.

[My people. I am here to fulfill the visions that were passed down to us by the old ones. I'm here to use my power for the people. All of the people. Together we will bring a return to peace and prosperity. We all will return to the ceremonies, Išnáti Awíčalowaŋpi, Haŋbléčeyapiand the rest. Together we will use the old to be new.]

Nahan hečun'unk'un pi ki owayang unkiyotan pi kte.
[And we're gonna look incredible while we do it.]
WÓWAČHIŊTȞANKE: Boom!

(The heads of Mount Rushmore explode apart. Music plays.)

END OF PLAY

KAYLA JAMES

LARISSA FASTHORSE (Sicangu Lakota Nation) is a 2025 Guggenheim Fellow, 2020 MacArthur Fellow, professor of practice (literature) at Arizona State University's Department of English, award-winning writer/choreographer, and co-founder of Indigenous Direction, the nation's leading consulting company for Indigenous arts and audiences. Larissa's revised book of the beloved Jerome Robbins Broadway musical, *Peter Pan*, toured nationally and internationally. She made her Broadway debut in the 2022–23 season with her satirical comedy, *The Thanksgiving Play*, making her the first known female Native playwright to be produced on Broadway. *The Thanksgiving Play* is one of the most-produced plays in America and abroad with over three hundred separate productions. Additional produced plays include *Fake It Until You Make It*; *For The People, The Democracy Project*; *What Would Crazy Horse Do?*; *Landless*; *Cow Pie Bingo*; *Average Family*; *Teaching Disco Squaredancing to Our Elders: a Class Presentation*; *Fancy Dancer*; and *Cherokee Family Reunion*. She develops work with the top theaters in the nation including Center Theatre Group, The Public, Second Stage, Yale Rep, Cornerstone, and Arena Stage.

MICHAEL JOHN GARCÉS is a recipient of the Doris Duke Artist, Princess Grace Statue, and Alan Schneider Director Awards. He is a professor of practice in the Department of English at Arizona State University. Michael served as artistic director of Cornerstone Theater Company, a professional community-engaged ensemble based in Los Angeles, where he directed new plays by many authors including Juliette Carrillo, Alison Carey, Larissa FastHorse, Naomi Iizuka, Lisa Loomer, and Mark Valdez. Cornerstone also produced several of his plays, including *Los Illegals*, *Magic Fruit*, *The Forked Path*, and *36 Yesses*. Other companies he has worked at include Arena Stage, Brooklyn Academy of Music, Carnegie Hall, Center Theatre Group (Mark Taper Forum), Geffen Playhouse, the Guthrie, INTAR, Kennedy Center, Mixed Blood, New York Theatre Workshop, Profile Theatre, Theatre Horizon, and Yale Rep. Michael is an alumnus of New Dramatists and was a longtime company member at Woolly Mammoth. He serves as executive vice president of the board of SDC, the national labor union representing professional stage directors and choreographers across the United States.